Praise for *Restoring the Lord's Day*

"Here is a richly textured book by someone who remembers, through the Catholic culture of New Orleans, rhythms that the rest of us never experienced. In fact, I think I am one of those suffering from some of the acedia diagnosed by Daniel Fitzpatrick. Even as I love being Catholic, I yearn for a deeper immersion in the joy of faith in all aspects of my existence. This book offers a window—rightly thought-provoking and controversial—into such a richer life."

—Matthew Levering,
James N. Jr. and Mary D. Perry Chair of Theology,
Mundelein Seminary

"With unmatched clarity and wisdom, Daniel Fitzpatrick reveals the many resplendent facets of the Lord's Day, guiding us from lost to found, and we recover a bit of ourselves along the way. Midway through my reading, I decided it would be my book on hand during Lent. Its message of poignant and efficacious beauty shows us that even the small moments of the day can be given to the Lord. This work will be a dear companion as we live out the liturgical calendar in ourselves, in our reflections, and with our families. *Restoring the Lord's Day* is its own high poetics of the spaces given to God."

—Caitlin Smith Gilson,
Professor of Philosophy, University of Holy Cross,
and Associate Editor, *The New Ressourcement Journal*

"Man lives by the sweat of his brow but is born for leisure. Human happiness consists of peace and stillness, and yet, as Pascal once observed, we become miserable at the thought of sitting in a room alone. Our days are filled with the hum of activity, and yet our true destiny is contemplation. In this marvelous essay, Daniel Fitzpatrick renews and deepens the call of Josef Pieper to restore a true vision of human nature and our calling to leisure, stillness, and contemplation. It is at once an explanatory critique of a wayward modern age and a wide-ranging, richly detailed invitation to reorder our world and our lives to conform to the essentially liturgical structure of reality. In brief, we cannot be fully ourselves unless we restore once again the beauty and stillness of the Lord's Day."

—James Matthew Wilson,
Author of *The Vision of the Soul*

"*Restoring the Lord's Day* offers the clearest antidote to our modern ADHD-narcissistic-frenetic restlessness: proper worship of God and reestablishing the Sabbath. This book will help you see that nothing is more important because if we understand worship, then everything else will fall into its proper place. Daniel Fitzpatrick is a master of words and has written a treasure. Enjoy the depth and care in these pages, as you learn to let go of acedia's grip."

—Dr. Mario Sacasa, LMFT,
Host of the *Always Hope* podcast

"*Tolle lege! Restoring the Lord's Day* is delightful and challenging—a tour de force that diagnoses the malignancy of acedia wreaking havoc on Christian festivity. Daniel Fitzpatrick unveils the hidden connections between technology and torpor, usury and anxiety, sex and sadness—deadly fruits of acedia's root. Weaving together the wisdom of Shakespeare and Dante, Ratzinger and John Paul II, Maria von Trapp and F. Scott Fitzgerald into a rich tapestry, Ftizpatrick helps us to recognize our sickness. But not satisfied to diagnose the patient, *Restoring the Lord's Day* offers eucharistic antidotes to the poisons of our age, practical suggestions for families seeking to recover the abiding joy of worshipping the Lord and to live by the light of the Lamb.

—Dr. Joshua Brumfield
Author of *The Benedict Proposal*

Restoring the Lord's Day

Daniel Fitzpatrick

RESTORING THE LORD'S DAY

How Reclaiming Sunday Can Revive Our Human Nature

SOPHIA INSTITUTE PRESS
Manchester, New Hampshire

Sophia Institute Press
Box 5284, Manchester, NH 03108
1-800-888-9344
www.SophiaInstitute.com

Sophia Institute Press is a registered trademark of Sophia Institute.

paperback ISBN 978-1-64413-598-3

ebook ISBN 978-1-64413-599-0

Library of Congress Control Number: 2024932753

First printing

For Grace

Contents

Loomings, or How This Came to Be

One day during my junior year of high school, I was at home, sick—just sick enough to avoid class, but well enough to enjoy myself. I read two plays during those blissful eight hours of silence. The first, Oscar Wilde's *The Importance of Being Earnest*, whet my appetite for heavier delights, and I turned next to *King Lear*. It was the first of Shakespeare's plays that I had picked up of my own volition, and I read it in one sitting, basking in a sense of accomplishing the real work of education there in my parents' recliner. Even today, my understanding of the play remains clouded, and no doubt a great deal of what Shakespeare was about simply washed over me that day, yet the text left behind certain indelible impressions: outrage at the disenfranchisement of Cordelia, Lear's virtuous daughter; grief at her death; and, above all, a sense that there, in pre-Arthurian Britain, the Bard had portrayed a world where things had gone badly wrong. Reading the play now, I find myself almost physically assaulted by this sense. Regan and Goneril, Lear's vicious daughters, first vie with each other for supreme sycophancy, then descend into what amounts to a kind of sinning spree, with hardly one of the Ten Commandments left unbroken in their wake. Edmund, too, as the primary antagonist, betrays

brother, father, king, counselor, and consort. Neither Gloucester—Edmund's father—nor King Lear himself can be considered
faultless, the former leaping too quickly to conclusions, the latter
abandoning his office and enacting his darker purpose to enjoy
a life of ease behind his boar hounds. Even Cordelia is not quite
blameless. The initial "nothing" with which she greets her aged
father's request for an account of her love rings, at worst, of a kind
of perversity, and at best of a shade of imprudence. There, in Lear's
Britain, no one is quite blameless, yet hardly anyone has eyes to see
the depth of horror into which their world has fallen. It is a place
in which the madman and the fool grope hand in hand toward
the truth of things, with the rest of the world stumbling about
in a darkness of its own creation. As Gloucester puts it, " 'Tis the
time's plague when madmen lead the blind."[1]

It occurs to me, too, that, in *King Lear*, Shakespeare has presented us with a world intensely familiar. Those who hold fast to
the gospel, to reason—to truth and goodness and beauty—are seen
as so many madmen raving over the face of the earth. Meanwhile, a
blood-dimmed tide of liberalism sweeps across the Western world,
with the proponents of wokeness preaching fervidly out of their
own blindness, having put out their own eyes of faith and reason.
Ours is, as Walker Percy puts it, a world where things have "gone
very wrong, indeed," apparently to a greater degree even than the
typical wrongness that's stalked mankind since Eden.[2]

---

[1] Shakespeare, *King Lear*, 4.1.46. References are to act, scene, and
line.

[2] Walker Percy, "Diagnosing the Modern Malaise," in *Signposts in a
Strange Land*, ed. Patrick Samway (New York: Farrar, Straus, and
Giroux, 1991), 206. For "blood-dimmed tide," see William Butler
Yeats, "The Second Coming."

I confess, though, that even as a boy of sixteen, I had little sense of the depth of our world's hurt. I knew in an academic sense, of course, of the Shoah and Hiroshima, of Dresden and Rwanda, of abortion and euthanasia. I had seen New Orleans' housing projects and heard of her murders, but my own day-to-day experience was, thanks to my family and its New Orleanian and Catholic roots, highly insular. Our family life hinged on Sunday Mass at Immaculate Conception Parish, just across Canal Street from the French Quarter. It is a stunningly beautiful church, with an altar that won first prize at a Paris World Exhibition and a sculpture of the Virgin commissioned long ago by the French monarchy. It taught me early the critical lesson that the nearer one sits to the altar, the higher one sees into the dome. It was a wonderful place to worship, and everything else in our family life, though I was scarcely aware of the fact, flowed from those Masses.

The *joie de vivre* which was so closely allied to the liturgical rhythm of life in New Orleans became the pattern of my consciousness of the world. After Mass, we would go for a leisurely walk in City Park, eating warm, sugared beignets along the way. After Christmas came the Mardi Gras season and an Ash Wednesday whose meaning was clear to just about everyone in the city. After the Good Friday Nine Churches Walk and Easter came hurricane season, when, each year, we knew we stood to lose everything. There beats in New Orleans a cultural rhythm such as I have found in no other American city, a rhythm ultimately founded on the city's Catholic identity. To a large degree, it was this rhythm which concealed from me the fact that most of the world had fallen into a pulseless facsimile of eternity, a relentless grind, day after day, week after week, on and on without respite or festivity.

Well do I recall my first Mardi Gras as an undergraduate at the University of Dallas, a place which, though dear to my heart, seemed on that gray February day to become a dismal place. What pagan land had I entered where Fat Tuesday was borne as doggedly as any other American Tuesday? But even pagans had their festivals. What godless, ultra-modern landscape had I come to inhabit?

Despite this, in the main, my university years were proof against the ills of the world, thanks be to God. Several years would pass after my graduation before I myself came to feel some of the dead nausea of postmodernity. Nonetheless, it was during my senior year of philosophy studies, in a seminar on melancholy, depression, and other shades of sadness, that I was handed a critical clue to the sort of reflection which has ultimately issued in this book. Our seminar director, Dr. Philip Rosemann, said the Sabbath has ceased to exist. This, of course, is no secret. Indeed, it is so manifestly obvious, and has been throughout my lifetime, that it had never occurred to me even to note it. But it bears noting indeed. We no longer honor the Sabbath. True, the churches are open. True, the banks are closed. True, more people are free to rest on Sundays than during the rest of the week. Long gone are the days, though, when all the shops were shut and all the churches were filled in the morning, when the afternoons meant lingering around the dinner table, reading, telling stories, making music—in short, enjoying a contemplative rest in the presence of the Lord and fellow men.

Dr. Rosemann's comment also prompted certain vague observations to begin to crystallize in my mind. Throughout my childhood, ideal as it was in many ways, I had nonetheless noticed that Sundays were home to some of the most anxious moments in the week. It was as though any stress I felt from school mounted to a climax sometime between three o'clock and bedtime on Sunday, and then it slowly declined over the course of the week, reaching a low when I arrived home on Friday afternoon. Nor was I alone in this experience. My grandmother had often expressed to me her own Sunday sadness, a feeling rooted in part in the long-past memories of her late husband, who operated the concessions in New Orleans' City Park, always having to work on Sundays. My mother, too, seemed to grow more anxious as Sunday wound toward evening.

There is nothing surprising about this anxiety, nor is being anxious in itself a sign of failing to be present to God in the way that Sunday calls us to be. We will discuss later how even the Lord, having commanded us to be anxious about nothing, was Himself intensely anxious in the Garden of Gethsemane. Indeed, having warned us to be anxious about nothing, it was precisely nothing, the vast nothingness of sin, of human life divorced from the Father's love, that caused His anxiety.

For us, striving even as we are to follow the narrow way, ~~how often is it the case that our anxiety is in fact a mark of a failure to rest in the Lord?~~ This became clearer to me when, in my undergraduate senior thesis, I wrote about acedia, or sloth, and its relation to the dark night of the soul—as if God is no longer present to us. In reading about acedia, though, and its love of distraction, its weariness with occupations and friends and colleagues, in hearing accounts of fourth-century desert monks afflicted by the "noonday devil," I felt as though I were reading a report from the desert of my own soul.

I was surprised to learn that many modern authors, including Evelyn Waugh and Karl Barth, have named acedia the besetting sin of the modern age. I was surprised to learn, too, that ~~St. Thomas Aquinas said that sloth is a sin directly opposed to the precept to hallow the Sabbath.~~ I remembered Dr. Rosemann's comment, and I began to wonder at this connection between sloth, the evacuation of the Sabbath as a cultural phenomenon, and our failure as a people to take up the way of prayer commended to us by mystics of all ages. How did this all hang together? Why were sloth and the Sabbath connected? And why had this connection apparently been brought raging to the forefront of our modern spiritual climate?

A possible answer, and a further clue to the composition of this book, arose when I reread St. Augustine's *Confessions*, having moved back to New Orleans and taken a teaching post at my alma mater, Jesuit High School. There, in book 11, I came as if for the first time upon St. Augustine's discussion of time. He defines it as nothing more than a distension of the mind, a being drawn apart, an inability to rest in the present as we are dragged by memory into the past and into the future by anticipation.[3] Here, then, was what seemed a precise psychological account of my own experience of the Lord's Day: worrying over the failures of Friday and the challenges of Monday.

For Augustine, though, the stakes are more than merely psychological; on a personal level, they are eschatological—that is, intrinsically connected to our final end. For if Heaven is nothing other than eternal presence to God, and if we allow our temporal anxiety so effectively to draw us out of God's peaceful presence now, how can we possibly expect to be prepared for an eternity of that presence?

It seemed to me, then, that here was the crux of the matter, the critical psychological dynamic at work in evacuating the Lord's Day of its meaning as the temporal touch point for man on the way. We have lost true Sabbath observance, fulfilled in Sunday worship and contemplative rest, because of acedia, and the human tendency toward acedia has been exacerbated by the anxiety that attends our being drawn apart in time.

What, then, has made our particular age so prone to this temporal distension and thus to acedia? What has caused us to forget

---

[3] St. Augustine, *Confessions*, bk. 11.

the Lord's Day? This book seeks answers to these questions and, what is ultimately more important, attempts to set forth measures whereby the Body of Christ may live the Lord's Day on earth as a means of bringing about the Kingdom.

Our task, in short, could be summarized thus: to see how our world has lost the truth of Lord's Day festivity (not for lack of try-ing, as the catalogue of "National Days," from National Cherry Pie Day to National Package Protection Day to National Stay Home Because You're Well Day, hilariously attests), and to suggest means for restoring Sunday as the earthly heart of human happiness.

I will leave the rest for the text proper, but not without first offering a word on method, for which an apology—in both senses of the word—may be due.

It will perhaps have become clear from the few preceding para-graphs that my bent is for the philosophical, psychological, and literary rather than the scientific, my academic training having primarily been in classical philosophy and literature. The times demand data, and I have attempted to supply these wherever the need arises. Yet I admit a measure of skepticism on the usefulness of studies and surveys, on both theoretical and experiential grounds. Very briefly, the data produced by polls and surveys seem to me to bear the mark of the Marxist drive toward the class as the standard of measurement for human life and activity. Following Vico, the philosopher of the Italian Enlightenment, modern science declares that we can only truly know what we have made.[4] Hence, true knowledge is dependent upon the infinitely repeatable process of experimentation. The method is immensely useful, and, as far as

---

[4] Joshua Brumfield, *The Benedict Proposal: Church as Creative Minority in the Thought of Pope Benedict XVI* (Eugene, OR: Pickwick Publica-tions, 2020), 14-15.

it goes, it is nothing new either. Aristotle, in many of his activities, was with the modern scientist in taking interest in many individuals for the sake of deriving universals. What Aristotle also saw, though, and what we tend to dismiss as so much mythic nonsense, is the truth that the universal may be known not only by way of many individuals, but also by way of one individual.

The modern method thereby tends to get things backward where man is concerned, treating him merely as a kind of thing that can therefore be divided into classes according to skin color, creed, political affiliation, level of education, and so on, usually for some political aim.

As Christians, though, our concern is always for the individual man and his capacity to live as a member of the Body of the Son of Man himself. Data, useful as they may at times be, can hardly convert man to accept the share in Sonship offered to him. Surveys and polls may help to contribute to a shift in mindset which then gives space for conversion to take place, but conversion itself is always the result of a personal encounter with Christ. That is, what is most profoundly important in human life is the anecdotal. St. Paul spread the gospel with such zeal for one reason only: something had happened to him, and he had to tell the world about it. There was no other way left for him.

Among the great losses of modernity has been a precipitous decline in our capacity to encounter others as individuals, which I again perceive to flow from the seductions of Marx's co-option of the Hegelian dialectic. Hegel understood history as a process of development wherein contrary forces produced new syntheses of thought and spirit as the life of the Trinity unfolded in the world. Marx secularized this process and cast it in terms of an endless class struggle. It is partially in view of this manner of separating people into classes that we no longer encounter other men and women as materially unique creatures who, for all their uniqueness, are nonetheless directed formally—that is, universally—to their Creator as their proper end. We rather encounter them as Republican or Democrat, black or white, socialist or capitalist. The other becomes either an asset in the development of my own self through the assertion of my will, or he becomes an obstacle. As Stratford Caldecott has put it, following the insistence of John Paul II on the primacy of the personal encounter as the locus of grace, "We are used to thinking in geopolitical terms, in statistics and mass movements. The pope asks us to believe instead that what is most important in the world and in history lies in the smallest and most intimate details: the glance, the smile, the encounter with another person."[5]

With an eye to turning our attention back to the value of the individual as the locus of encounter with the universal, I have therefore in many cases availed myself not of the statisticians but of the poets, calling on Homer, Dante, Fitzgerald, Pound, Percy, and others to illustrate those truths of human existence which can best be known by coming to know particular men and women. Ours is an age that denigrates fiction (and this in itself points to our failure to worship, to rest, to be properly festive, for, as Josef Pieper notes, "Wherever assent to the world is expressly rejected ... the root of both festivity and the arts is destroyed"),[6] yet it is also partly due to our failure to produce good fiction and our further failure to read good fiction that we have lost our capacity for encountering the other as a creature meant for life with the Creator. Bad fiction, of

---

[5] Stratford Caldecott, *Not as the World Gives: The Way of Creative Justice* (Kettering, OH: Second Spring, 2014), 147.

[6] Josef Pieper, *In Tune with the World: A Theory of Festivity* (South Bend, IN: St. Augustine's Press, 1999), 56.

the sort popular with the modern liberal, is little more than propaganda. Characters are developed as vehicles for promoting social programs or as representatives of oppressed or oppressing classes. Such works should indeed be ignored. Yet the example of many of the greatest philosophers and theologians, from Plato and Aristotle to Augustine and Aquinas to Heidegger and Kant, argues for the propriety of turning to the poets as champions of the truth of human existence and, furthermore, as artisans of the words whereby we may come to know the Word. When a story is told truly, when words are used truly, they cannot fail to lead us into an encounter with the Word. And when a character is portrayed truthfully, he or she becomes, for the reader, a conduit for an encounter with Christ, either by displaying what it is to become more fully human and thus more like Christ, or by demonstrating the pain of the only loss that, in the end, is real: that of not becoming a saint.

To engage in criticism of one's own time is at best a delicate matter. Facile judgments are forever at hand, and, in general, it may be surmised that the great seers of the day have not arisen, or not been recognized, until long after the day is done and a new age has taken its place, fraught with its own ills, its own questions. Moreover, immured in the scientific method as we are, we have lost much of the art of criticism. We are like those crowds Jesus decries for their ability to read the weather but their inability to read the signs of the times. Nonetheless, it belongs to those of an age to feel its peculiar quality, to bear the existential weight of that sense that something—perhaps something we cannot quite name as yet—has gone badly wrong. In a time and a country where leisure is available to a degree unimaginable to many of our forebears, we have somehow persisted in denying ourselves true leisure, true rest. We have become so many pharaohs to ourselves. And here, with this clue, we make our beginning.

1

Sloth and the Loss of the Lord's Day

From the time that Israel began its sojourn in Egypt until its liberation under Moses, although God's Chosen People were not in the land that was their inheritance through Abraham, they seem to have experienced something of the blessing meant for man in the beginning, when God called Adam to be fruitful and multiply. Thanks to Joseph's divine gifts and prudential judgment, Israel enjoyed special favor in Egypt, and they "multiplied and became so very numerous that the land was filled with them" (Exod. 1:7). Indeed, during the time of Joseph's ministry, it was the Egyptians who sold their land and made themselves Pharaoh's slaves in order to escape the ravages of famine (Gen. 47:19–21).

Then a new king arose in Egypt. This man knew nothing of Joseph, and he oppressed the Israelites, forcing them to build new garrisons using brick and mortar, the implements of Babel (Gen. 11:3). But God heard the cry of His people. And when God sent Moses as an instrument of Israel's deliverance from bondage in Egypt, Moses did not ask Pharaoh merely to let the people go. He asked rather that Israel be allowed to *worship*. The exchange between the prophet and the king set the stage for the drama of the heart that would play out between the Lord and His people down to our day:

Moses and Aaron went to Pharaoh and said, "Thus says the LORD, the God of Israel: Let my people go, that they may hold a feast for me in the wilderness."

Pharaoh answered, "Who is the LORD, that I should obey him and let Israel go? I do not know the LORD, and I will not let Israel go."

They replied, "The God of the Hebrews has come to meet us. Let us go a three days' journey in the wilderness, that we may offer sacrifice to the LORD, our God, so that he does not strike us with the plague or the sword."

The king of Egypt answered them, "Why, Moses and Aaron, do you make the people neglect their work? Off to your labors!" (Exod. 5:1–4)

Israel had prospered in Egypt. They had grown from a tribe to a vast assembly which would become a nation. Yet it was not for any greatness on their part that God desired to deliver them. Nor was God's project simply to free the people for their own pursuits. They were instead the people whom God had called to be His own, the people who, since the time of Abraham, had established altars and offered sacrifice to God, the people through whom all the world would be called back to its original glory as the space in which worship is offered to God the Creator. Israel's proper liberty was not freedom *from* bondage, but freedom *for* worship.[7]

Pharaoh did not know the Lord. And, in Moses' request that Israel be allowed to worship, Pharaoh saw only an admission of laziness. In his eyes, a desire to worship this nameless God could

---

[7] See Joseph Cardinal Ratzinger, *The Spirit of the Liturgy*, trans. John Saward (San Francisco: Ignatius Press, 2014), 16.

only be an attempt to escape from the labor that constituted the worship of Pharaoh. And so he redoubled the labors of the people, commanding that they fill the same quota of bricks but without being supplied the straw for the work. The Israelite taskmasters were beaten and complained to Pharaoh. When he refused to relent, the people complained to Moses, incensed that he, with his message from God, had made them odious to Pharaoh. And Moses cried out to God as well, praying for the people's relief.

Thus the fundamental choice was set before Israel, one which would be brought into focus at the establishment of the covenant on Sinai: Would they serve Pharaoh, or would they serve God?[8] Would they persist in fashioning bricks—the six-sided building blocks of Babel that would harden in the sun as did Pharaoh's heart in the light of God's will—or would they themselves become, in time, a living temple of the Lord?

The drama of this choice may feel far-off to those of us occupying the latter-day, Christ-haunted Western world.[9] Especially in America, where the love of freedom remains keen and where, bureaucracy notwithstanding, our wills are mostly left unfettered, we little sense the intensity of Pharaoh's hold over us. We imagine ourselves beholden to no one, completely open to the luxurious possibilities of modern existence. We little suspect that we ourselves have become as pharaohs, exercising a shrewd tyranny over our own hearts as we grow less and less free to worship God.

---

[8] Ibid., 19-23.
[9] See Walker Percy, *Love in the Ruins: The Adventures of a Bad Catholic at a Time Near the End of the World* (New York: Farrar, Straus, and Giroux, 1971). Throughout this book I employ echoes of phrases used by poets and novelists who have seen the nature of modern man's plight.

The Lord's Day Lost

In the desert, having come out of Egypt at last, the people were called back to engagement with God according to the original order of the world. Leaving Pharaoh behind was not enough. If it was to survive as a nation marked out by God, Israel had to learn to offer proper worship.[10] God had established the universe as a cosmic temple where leviathan would sport in the deep, lions would roar for prey, and the moon would mark the seasons—all as man gave praise.[11] Abraham, Isaac, and Jacob had gone about the land into which God called them, establishing altars to the Lord. Later, the Israelite people's desert wandering was a process of learning to worship anew. This involved not only the establishment of sacred places, such as Sinai or the tabernacle, which became its mobile analog, or even the Temple that Solomon would one day build. Israel had to recall that time itself is the medium of God's expression of love for man and that the rhythms of time reveal something of God's plan for human existence on earth.[12] And so the life of the nation became marked by festival seasons and by the injunction to honor the Sabbath, to rest from labor on the seventh day in imitation of the God who Himself rested on the seventh day of Creation. Freedom from Pharaoh meant freedom from those labors that prevent man from walking with God, from being present to Him in that contemplative joy in which the human heart is called to rest. Our lives are not our own. They flow from God

---

[10] See Ratzinger, *Spirit of the Liturgy*, 16. Thus it was not sufficient for just the men, or the people without the cattle, to go out of Egypt, for they did not know yet what the Lord would demand in worship.

[11] See Psalm 104.

[12] Hans Urs von Balthasar, *Heart of the World*, trans. Erasmo S. Leiva (San Francisco: Ignatius Press, 1979), 21–24.

and are oriented back toward Him, and we find no peace until we rest in the God who is our end.[13]

Our age refuses more and more to rest in the Lord. America, though professedly one of the most religious of the world's nations, has seen a steep decline in worship in the last century. Practically all available metrics indicate an American descent into secularism which shows little sign of relenting. A 2018 Gallup poll showed that while roughly 75 percent of American Catholics attended church weekly in 1955, the figure had declined to just 39 percent in 2014–2017.[14] The trend is not restricted to Catholics. A 2021 poll found that while some 70 percent of Americans belonged to a particular church for most of the twentieth century, fewer than half of Americans are church members today, largely because of the increase in religious "nones," those who hold no specific faith.[15] According to a recent Pew study, nearly a third of Americans are religiously unaffiliated, while the number of Americans who identify as Christian has declined some 10 percent in just the last decade.[16]

This is not news; we could add to these figures, in depressing succession, statistics on the decline in enrollment in Catholic

[13] See St. Augustine, *Confessions*, 3.

[14] Lydia Saad, "Catholics' Church Attendance Resumes Downward Slide," Gallup, April 9, 2018, https://news.gallup.com/poll/232226/church-attendance-among-catholics-resumes-downward-slide.aspx.

[15] Jeffrey M. Jones, "U.S. Church Membership Falls Below Majority for First Time," Gallup, March 29, 2021, https://news.gallup.com/poll/341963/church-membership-falls-below-majority-first-time.aspx.

[16] Gregory A. Smith, "About Three-in-Ten U.S. Adults Are Now Religiously Unaffiliated," Pew Research Center, December 14, 2021, https://www.pewresearch.org/religion/2021/12/14/about-three-in-ten-u-s-adults-are-now-religiously-unaffiliated/.

schools, the closure of parishes, the falling number of Catholics who believe in Christ's presence in the Eucharist, and even the swelling percentage of Americans who no longer believe in God at all.[17]

The statistics on faith in America can perhaps best be encapsulated by a simple observation of what our Sundays have come to look like; namely, they look like practically every other day. Perhaps the traffic is lighter. Perhaps the parks and zoos and lakefronts are somewhat more crowded. Perhaps the stock exchange is closed. Yet the steady golden roar of American commerce beats on as shoppers walk the malls, diners crowd the restaurants, and the checkout lines stretch as far as those for Holy Communion.

In his 2004 essay, "The Church as Culture," Robert Louis Wilken gave pointed voice to the way modern America has desacralized time: "Take, for example, the calendar. I am not thinking primarily of Santa displacing the Christ child or the Easter Bunny replacing the Resurrection; nor do I mean the transfer of festivals that fall in midweek (e.g., Epiphany or Pentecost or All Saints) to the nearest Sunday. I mean the dramatic, wholesale evacuation of Sunday as a holy day. At eleven o'clock on Sunday morning at Home Depot or Lowe's the lines of folks with cans of paint, two-by-fours, and joint cement stretch almost as far as they do on a Saturday morning."[18]

---

[17] Cf. Walker Percy, *The Moviegoer* (New York: A. Knopf, 1967), in which Binx Bolling muses on the 98 percent of Americans who believe in God and thus would seem to have everything figured out. Compare also the 1956 poll by Lou Harris finding that 97 percent of Americans believe in God, a number which had declined to 86 percent in 2014.

[18] Robert Louis Wilken, "The Church as Culture," *First Things*, April 2004, https://www.firstthings.com/article/2004/04/the-church-as-culture.

We have gone a long way further down the secular road in the two decades since Wilken decried our abnegation of the command to keep holy the Sabbath. In our time, a business's decision to shut its doors on Sunday meets with consternation and incredulity. Chick-fil-A, the wildly popular port of Southern hospitality, has made Lord's Day observance part of its brand. On highway exit signs all across America, the white chicken emblem stands almost entirely alone in proclaiming, "Closed on Sundays." And many of us driving by, whether commuting to our own Sunday labor or traveling home from a vacation aimed at forgetting for a moment the stresses of the week, scratch our heads in astonishment. How dare they close on Sundays, we wonder.

It's not that the endless commercial week merely encourages the shopping and dining which have become characteristic Sunday activities for many Americans. It also demands that many people go into work on Sunday as on any other day. The Bureau of Labor Statistics reports that roughly one-third of all Americans work on weekends and holidays.[19] For many, then, Sunday is just another node in the continuum of laborious days, stretching on in a kind of false eternity toward the end of life.

Even for those who neither work on Sundays nor engage in a great deal of activity, the festive meaning of the day has more and more evaporated. Many Catholics take Saturday evening vigil Masses as an opportunity to get the obligation over with in order to have an unencumbered Sunday dedicated to the grill and the TV screen. On Sundays during football season, churches are awash in the colors of the home team, and parishioners and pastors

---

[19] See table 2 in Bureau of Labor Statistics news release "American Time Use Survey—2022 Results," June 22, 2023, https://www.bls.gov/news.release/pdf/atus.pdf.

anxiously check their watches during the Consecration, wondering whether or not they'll make it home in time for kickoff and a long afternoon before the altar of Foot-Baal.[20]

There is something else afoot, though. It is not just that Sunday is no longer a font of spiritual refreshment born of loving communion with the God who is always attending to man. Rather, for many Americans, Sunday has become a moment of anxiety, teetering on the brink of Monday and the next yawning week of labor. As the Lord's Day draws on toward evening, social media threads become rife with laments, often couched in darkly comic terms, for the "Sunday scaries," which an article from the Cleveland Clinic describes as "feelings of intense anxiety and dread that routinely occur every Sunday." The article goes on to note that these feelings "often start in the late afternoon and continue into the evening. However, depending on a person's level of anxiety, these feelings can start as soon as they get out of bed."[21] In view of this anxiety, once our obligatory hour of worship is checked off, we tend to spend Sunday in pursuit of distraction.

We no longer honor the Sabbath. And Sunday, which fulfills the Sabbath,[22] has thus become dreadful. No longer are we present to the God who from the beginning is present to us. But how did we come to this cultural pass? It is one thing to observe that the Lord's Day has passed out of observance. It is another to try to say why—why has this deep malaise come upon us? Put another way, is there a particular sin under whose sway our culture has

---

[20] My thanks to Matthew Kuizon of Jesuit High School, Tampa, for this joke.

[21] "What Are the 'Sunday Scaries'?" Cleveland Clinic, December 7, 2021, https://health.clevelandclinic.org/sunday-scaries/.

[22] Pope John Paul II, Apostolic Letter on Keeping the Lord's Day Holy *Dies Domini* (May 31, 1998), no. 18.

fallen, a sin which, by its very nature, strikes at the Sabbath call to rest in the Lord?

A Brief History of Sloth

Evelyn Waugh, in his review of J. F. Powers's *Prince of Darkness and Other Stories*, called the collection

> a magnificent study of sloth—a sin which has not attracted much attention of late and which, perhaps, is the besetting sin of the age. Catholic novelists have dealt at length with lust, blasphemy, cruelty and greed—these provide obvious dramatic possibilities. We have been inclined to wink at sloth; even, in a world of go-getters, almost to praise it. An imaginative writer has advantages over the preacher and Mr. Powers exposes this almost forgotten, widely practiced, capital sin, in a way which brought an alarming whiff of brimstone to the nostrils of at least one reader.[23]

It's a striking claim, that sloth should be "the besetting sin of the age." Our day, far from being idle, inclines to a frantic industry, as Waugh notes in describing this "world of go-getters." Moreover, lust and avarice both seem more likely claimants to the throne of modern sinfulness, given our hypersexualized commercialism. Surely, too, we are more gluttonous than slothful, with our fast foods and our processed sugars and our American obesity. How can sloth possibly be the most pernicious of our troubles?

These diagnoses remain obscure until we begin to study the history of sloth, a sin perhaps better understood by the term *acedia*,

---

[23] Quoted in Daniel McInerny, "Sloth: The Besetting Sin of the Age?" *Logos: A Journal of Catholic Thought and Culture* 12, no. 1 (Winter 2009): 38-61.

a sin which the desert fathers associated with the "noonday devil" of Psalm 91.[24]

John Cassian, a fourth-century monk and one of the exponents of monasticism in the West, paid keen attention to the obstacles that monks face on the path of perfection. In his youth, he journeyed from present-day France to Palestine, where he took monastic orders in Bethlehem before undertaking a long sojourn among the desert monks in Egypt. There he witnessed firsthand the great power of acedia, known as the noonday devil quite literally because of its tendency to grip monks around the noon hour. He describes it thus in *The Foundations of the Cenobitic Life*:

> Our sixth combat is with what the Greeks call acedia, which we may term weariness or distress of heart. This is akin to dejection, and is especially trying to solitaries, and a dangerous and frequent foe to dwellers in the desert; and especially disturbing to a monk about the sixth hour, like some fever which seizes him at stated times, bringing the burning heat of its attacks on the sick man at usual and regular hours.[25]

Acedia, as Cassian observed it, was not simply laziness. It came upon monks as it comes upon us: as a deep sadness of heart, a shaft of the enemy deployed at the same hours so that the one afflicted had to contend not only with the pain of dejection but with the expectation that, as the sun rose to its zenith, the attack

---

[24] The formulation "noonday devil" is the rendering of the Vulgate by St. Jerome, which is preserved in the Douay-Rheims translation (Ps. 90:6) but is rendered otherwise in all other modern translations: e.g., "the plague that ravages at noon" (Ps. 91:6, NABRE).

[25] Quoted in Jennifer Radden, ed., *The Nature of Melancholy: From Aristotle to Kristeva* (Oxford: Oxford University Press, 2000), 71.

was on its way. Such anticipation itself heightens the piquancy of the devil's ploy.

Cassian goes on to indicate the behaviors acedia manifests, and again, his description of the desert monks under the sway of sloth illuminates much of our present society's behavior:

> And when this has taken possession of some unhappy soul, it produces dislike of the place, disgust with the cell, and disdain and contempt of the brethren who dwell with him or at a little distance.... It also makes the man lazy and sluggish about all manner of work.... Then besides this he looks about anxiously this way and that, and sighs that none of his brethren come to see him, and often goes in and out of his cell, and frequently gazes up at the sun, as if it was too slow in setting.[26]

Already a portrait is emerging of a kind of sin we know so familiarly that we have ceased even to see it as sin. The noonday devil drove Cassian's monks from their cells, whether in imagination or in fact, in search of some better way of serving God. But, contrary to this noonday inclination, we know that the monastic cell is objectively the locus of the monk's labor, the particular place in which he is vocationally called to know, love, and serve God. While ours is no society of monks, we nonetheless occupy similar vocational cells today. Perhaps we have many cells: the cells of our jobs, of our marriages, of our roles as parents, not to mention the cells of our cities and our churches and our very times. How often do we grow bored at work and wander the office in search of a fellow in boredom? How often do marriages end in divorce, or how often are spouses ignored in favor of television screens

[26] Ibid.

or social media feeds? How often are children told, "I can't play right now—I'm too busy," when the business at hand is simply reading the news, being distracted by things happening across the globe? How often are the pews empty, or how often do we go roving in search of the perfect parish where we can serve God to the height of our potential, rather than serving him right where we are? How often is time itself too slow? We may even frequently find ourselves in the position of Satan at the outset of the book of Job, walking back and forth upon the earth, and going up and down upon it (1:7).

If Cassian's observations on acedia help to shed light on our own cultural malaise, St. Thomas Aquinas provides even keener clues to perceiving the link between acedia and the desacralization of the Lord's Day. St. Thomas echoes Cassian in defining *acedia* as "sorrow in the Divine good about which charity rejoices."[27] He goes on to clarify that there are, as with all sins, degrees of slothfulness. If sloth moves a man only on the sensual level—that is, if it arises from the physical weariness of our proper labor but remains at the level of the senses, without compacting the assent of reason—it remains a venial sin. In similar manner, the sensual movement of lust remains venial if the mind does not consent to the bodily passion. On the other hand, when the body overwhelms the soul in sloth, and reason "consents in the dislike, horror and detestation of the Divine good," then sloth becomes mortal.[28]

Finally, and most critically for our purposes, Aquinas notes that sloth "is opposed to the precept about hallowing the Sabbath day. For this precept, in so far as it is a moral precept, implicitly

---

[27] St. Thomas Aquinas, *Summa Theologica* II–II, q. 35, art. 2, *Respondeo* ("I answer that …").

[28] Ibid., II–II, q. 35, art. 3, *Respondeo*.

commands the mind to rest in God: and sorrow of the mind about the Divine good is contrary thereto."[29] Here at last Waugh's assessment of modernity comes into sharper focus. Indeed, Waugh was keenly attuned to Aquinas's description of sloth, as he showed when, at the request of Ian Fleming, he wrote an essay on sloth for the *London Sunday Times*. "Man is made for joy in the love of God," he noted, "a love which he expresses in service. If he deliberately turns away from that joy, he is denying the purpose of his existence. The malice of Sloth lies not merely in the neglect of duty (though that can be a symptom of it) but in the refusal of joy. It is allied to despair."[30]

To Waugh's analysis we might add that man's most proper activity, the service he most firmly renders God, is worship in the Mass, where we offer God to God and we ourselves become tabernacles of the eucharistic Lord. If sloth is opposed to the worship we owe on the Lord's Day, then a culture that abandons the Lord's Day may well be convicted of sloth.

Aquinas and Waugh make an important distinction here in emphasizing that sloth is not sorrow or anxiety in a general sense but rather a detestation of the divine good. On a certain level, the anxiety that many of us feel on Sundays constitutes a natural response to some of the conditions of laboring in a fallen world. It is normal, that is, to feel a degree of stress over the weight of responsibilities. But that anxiety becomes characteristically slothful when it is directed to God Himself. The slothful person is anxious about the concrete circumstances of life, to be sure, but

---

[29] Ibid., reply to objection 1.

[30] Evelyn Waugh, "Sloth," *Sunday Times* (London), 1962, quoted in Heather Hughes, "An Unconditional Surrender: Evelyn Waugh on *Acedia*" in *Acedia*, ed. Heidi J. Hornik et al. (Waco, TX: Baylor University, 2013), 46.

only secondarily. His main hatred is for the divine will on which the contours of life are founded. Sunday worship calls for intimate contact with the divine good—indeed, in the profound fulfillment of the worship Israel offered in its desert tabernacle, the Mass calls man to become a tabernacle, to allow God to dwell in him eucharistically. What could be more odious to a soul that despises the divine good than to be made one with that good?

St. Thomas's point tallies well with the fact that our rejection of Sabbath worship is not because we lack time. While more and more people are working on Sundays, increased labor is not in itself the cause of decreased worship. It is not the case that people don't have time for worship, that our society lacks sufficient leisure for true worship to thrive. On the contrary, the average worker has far more leisure time today than he did in the nineteenth century. Whereas manufacturing laborers worked between sixty and seventy hours weekly in the 1800s, most Americans work between thirty-seven and forty-seven hours per week today and enjoy roughly five hours of daily leisure.[31] Though our time has been comparatively liberated, we refuse to rest in the divine good. Like Pharaoh, we refuse to know the Lord.

In his book, *Acedia and Its Discontents*, R. J. Snell makes the case that acedia's ascendancy over the modern soul is a product of hatred for the original goodness of God's creation.[32] In his assessment, Snell highlights the manner in which the reality of the world itself becomes repugnant to those steeped in sloth.[33] The desert

---

[31] Robert Whaples, "Hours of Work in U.S. History," Enconomic History Association, August 14, 2001, https://eh.net/encyclopedia/hours-of-work-in-u-s-history/.

[32] R. J. Snell, *Acedia and Its Discontents: Metaphysical Boredom in the Empire of Desire* (Kettering, OH: Angelico Press, 2015), 62ff.

[33] Ibid.

monks, when they capitulated to the noonday devil and refused to join with God in affirming the goodness of the order of things, longed to be in other places, among different fellows, performing different works; so does modern man despise his neighbors, his same tired commute, his coworkers, and the menial tasks that prevent his actually doing something worthwhile—which perhaps he could do, if only things were … different.

We have seen that Israel's journey away from Pharaoh required a return to the joyful worship that marked the cosmos in the beginning. Snell emphasizes the fact that acedia, in rejecting the order of things, the fundamental solidity of reality flowing from God's ongoing creative act, refuses to see with God that the world is good. In our day, when secular society sees the earth itself as the last endangered divinity and sees man as the scourge of nature, true worship is especially repugnant. Any attempt to view man in relation to a loving Creator demands that man be accorded his original dignity, a dignity the modern eco-religion refuses to grant.

Snell's focus on acedia's refusal to rejoice with Adam in the original goodness—to say, as Adam said to Eve, "At last!" in glad affirmation of God's work—further illustrates the way in which sloth constitutes a rejection of Sabbath rest. For God, in resting from His labors, did not cease the loving act of Creation.[34] His rest remains a delighted affirmation of the world, a constant mainte-nance of a world that remains good, however much acedia would have us feel otherwise.

In sum, three aspects of the noonday devil's approach will inform the rest of our study.

---

[34] St. Thomas Aquinas, *Summa Theologica* I, q. 73, art. 3.

First, sloth often takes bodily weariness as a point of entry. Fasting and laboring in the desert heat from early morning till noon left the ancient monks prone to the heartsick weariness that acedia inflicts. This bodily weariness then worked to gain the consent of reason in actively hating the divine good of the monk's vocation.

Second, sloth is not simply idleness or physical weariness but rather a loathing for man's proper end. Thus, sloth turns man away from his highest activity, which is also his most profound form of rest: contemplative presence to the God who is always present to creation.

Third, this loathing for man's highest good results in a disgust with creation and with the concrete circumstances of life wherein we are called to find God's will for us. This disgust extends to time itself, which is the medium in which God reveals himself to man.

We turn now to consider some further aspects of acedia, those qualities which make it especially pervasive and difficult to detect.

The Devil without a Shadow: The Subtlety of Sloth

The devil delights in going about unnoticed. He loves nothing more than to worm his way so insidiously into the fabric of our society that he may walk about in broad daylight unseen. And while some demons love the shadows, the noonday demon of sloth is abroad when the sun is right overhead, when time seems to stand still, when the shadows of things vanish. Sloth is among the least immediately recognizable sins, and, in a world where sin itself is ever more relegated to the trash heap of Western civilization (I note that even my word-processing software persists in trying to correct *sin* to *sun*), the noonday devil has seized his opportunity to extinguish the joyful worship which he has hated from the beginning.

We will look into some means of putting sloth to flight. Before that, though, it is worth considering certain features of sloth which make it so pervasive. The renowned medieval poet Dante Alighieri, for instance, found the battle with acedia so central to man's journey toward the empyrean that he placed the terrace of sloth midway up the mountain of Purgatory, almost precisely halfway through his journey across the cosmos.[35] While acedia is particularly dominant in our day, Dante's positioning it as he does indicates his sense that acedia, as a special sin against charity, presents a focal point of the evil one's attempts to turn us away from divine love. This is not to say that Dante considers sloth the worst of all sins. Pride, at the foot of the mountain of Purgatory, holds that position. Yet the pride of Satan and his betrayal of God—which, together, keep him cased in ice in the depths of Dante's Inferno—are akin to that sloth that hates the divine goodness of reality.[36]

Then, too, it is not only the monks and the Catholic poets who have witnessed to the poison of sloth. Concern over acedia can also be found in the Homeric roots of the Western tradition. Achilles, the great hero whose divine anger tipped the scales against the Trojans, exhibits many of the symptoms of sloth described by Cassian and Aquinas. When his concubine, Briseis, is stolen by Agamemnon, Achilles withdraws from battle and sulks beside the ships of the Myrmidons: "Achilles / weeping went and sat in sorrow apart from his companions / beside the beach of the grey sea looking out on the infinite water."[37] The Greeks fare poorly in his absence, and the Trojans nearly succeed in burning the famous thousand ships. Still, Achilles refuses to overcome his sorrow; despite the entreaties of his erstwhile friends, he continues to

---

[35] See Dante Alighieri, *Purgatorio*, vol. 2 of *The Divine Comedy*, trans. Daniel Fitzpatrick (St. Louis: En Route Books and Media, 2022), canto 17.

[36] See Dante Alighieri, *Inferno*, vol. 1 of *The Divine Comedy*, canto 23.

[37] Homer, *Iliad*, bk. 1, lines 348-350.

linger on the shore, soothing his heart with songs of heroes. He despises the kingly power that gives Agamemnon sway over the people. He detests the mere mortals around him. He longs for the far-off land of his father, where he might while away his days in peaceful farming, abandoning his brothers-in-arms to their fate.

Achilles's actions alone are enough to recall the behaviors of the desert monks, sighing and looking off into the distance, disgusted at the circumstances of their present lives. But, in his preface to an issue of *Logos* magazine, Michael C. Jordan notes Homer's use of a term which linguistically connects Achilles with what we know as sloth. Nestor, the aged horseman, describes Achilles as *ou kedetai*.[38] That is, Achilles has no care, and it is from the Greek *a-kedos*, lack of care, that we derive our word *acedia*. That Homer should apparently have intuited something of the immense power of acedia comes as no surprise. As Plato and Aristotle knew, the Homeric epics contained the germs of all later philosophy. Nonetheless, the continuity of experience running from Achilles through the desert monks to today's man in the office building gives startling testimony to the depth of acedia's roots.

Jordan argues further that Achilles's rejection of the highest goods of ancient Grecian society constitutes a further proof of the intensity of his sloth.[39] That is, Achilles's heartsick weariness stems largely from a disgust with the heroic desire for honor through martial prowess. As a demigod, such prowess is, in a sense, his calling—defeating the Trojans is what he was born for. But this is hateful to him now. Wouldn't it be better, after all, to live a long life in peace and solitude? Isn't honor in the hands of other men

---

[38] Michael C. Jordan, "Preface," *Logos: A Journal of Catholic Thought and Culture* 12, no. 1 (Winter 2009): 5.

[39] Ibid.

and thus not worth seeking, especially when the accidents of life and war often conduce to the honor of cowards and weaklings?

Achilles, as forefather of acedia, ultimately not only demonstrates the depth of sloth's hold on man but also elucidates one of the sin's most insidious features; namely, that it tends to afflict people who have chosen some kind of excellence, and it does so under the guise of calling them to further excellence.

Consider the desert monks. Whatever their failings, they had at some point opened themselves to a call to know the Lord intimately, to give up riches, wives, children, and lands in order to enter into earthly conversation with God as their preface to eternity with him. They had "chosen the better part" (Luke 10:42). And their sadness consisted in desiring to do more, to bear richer fruit, to be more spiritually productive. Thus, as Heather Hughes notes, "The fourth-century desert Christians told stories about slothful monks who did works of mercy in order to distract themselves from some greater good of prayer or service which they had come to abhor."[40] This desire for a better means of holiness than the one God desires for us is illusory, yet it flickers so distinctly about the margins of monastic life, like a mirage in the guise of a perfect monastery, as to bring about intense confusion. After all, no man is secure in his salvation until he has finished the race, and much of the path passes through darkness. The darkness of sloth is so deep because it does not try to replace the good of human existence with a lesser good like food or sex but rather causes us to loathe the good itself. This causes intense interior confusion, given that all men, according to Aristotle, desire the good. However misguided our notion of goodness might become, we tend to act in accordance with what we think is good. Part of the terror of

---

[40] Hughes, "An Unconditional Surrender," 46.

acedia is that, when we are in its grip, the greatest of goods no longer seems compelling.[41]

While the excellence of the present age stands in grave doubt, we may at least note that the majority of Americans are deeply concerned with morality. Many believe that America is in poor moral health, while roughly four in five say they are worried about the decline in American morals.[42] And, judging from the prevalence of virtue-signaling behavior in the public forum, from wearing the right protective equipment to posting the right memes to hanging the right signs on our doors, it matters a great deal to most of us that we be perceived as doing the good.

That said, having lost any normative sense of theology and anthropology, our morals are bathed in confusion. And sloth delights in the ensuing uncertainty, causing us to rush from one activity to the next, seeking desperately for the good without any sense of what that good might be. The slothful monk sought a place where he could encounter God more fully. The slothful man of modernity hides from God in the jungles of his cities and hopes only to encounter himself. And among those striving for holiness in the midst of modernity, the temptations of sloth are grave, urging us to hate our age entirely, to despise the efforts of those around us in their own labors, to wish so deeply for a better cultural milieu that we despair of the opportunities for charity before us.

---

[41] Indeed, as we shall see later, the confusion of sloth is in many ways similar to the confusion occasioned by the dark night of the soul. The slothful soul rejects divine love, whereas the soul in the dark night feels that that love has been withdrawn. In both instances, the soul encounters the feeling of having lost divine love.

[42] Frank Newport, "Untangling Americans' Complex Views of Morality," Gallup, June 17, 2022, https://news.gallup.com/opinion/polling-matters/393782/untangling-americans-complex-views-morality.aspx.

Sloth and the Loss of the Lord's Day

From Homer to Dante, from Cassian to Waugh, the poets and spiritual masters of all ages have called attention to this especially subversive sin. And not a few recent authors, Snell among them, have made compelling cases that sloth is indeed the besetting sin of the modern age. The rejection of the Lord's Day is perhaps the clearest proof of acedia's sway over modern man. Later, we will look to ways in which the Mass itself provides the purest antidote to sloth. Before that, though, we wish simply to observe two scriptural figures as models for overcoming acedia.

Contra Sloth: From Jacob to Christ

As Abraham went about the land of Canaan, the land to which the Lord had called him, he raised altars and dug wells. The universe is a cosmic temple, and man, whose end is to worship God, marks the world with places where fit offerings may be raised to the Almighty. He also works the earth, digging into its crust to strike the water that will sustain him and his flocks. Abraham modeled the pattern of praise and labor that would later be followed out in the Rule of St. Benedict and that is demanded of all those who walk with the Lord in faith.

To Isaac fell the task of unearthing many of the wells that his father Abraham had dug. And Isaac and his flocks multiplied greatly in the land of the Philistines.

Jacob, Isaac's son, having received Esau's birthright and Isaac's blessing, went forth to Haran in search of a wife. Jacob's acquaintance with God had not yet become personal, but when he lay down to sleep one night, with his head resting on a stone, he dreamed of angels ascending and descending on a ladder stretching into Heaven, and the Lord spoke to him and promised that his descendants would be numerous and would inherit the land of Canaan. Jacob's response on waking supplies a fitting model for man as he learns more and more to walk with God: "When Jacob awoke from his sleep, he said, 'Truly, the LORD is in this place and I did not know it!' He was afraid and said: 'How awesome this place is! This is nothing else but the house of God, the gateway to heaven!'" (Gen. 28:16-17).

Wherever we are, the Lord is in that place. So often, we know it not.

From that day, Jacob's life became a model of the sort of labor which overcomes sloth. He set up an altar and continued to the land of the Kedemites. In the middle of the day, around the time when the noonday devil stalks abroad, Jacob came upon a well in the open country, with several shepherds gathered around it. The well was covered with a stone so large that it could only be moved when all the local shepherds had assembled to water their flocks. Jacob, moved by the sight of his kinswoman Rachel, who was approaching with the flocks of her father, Laban, shifted the stone aside himself and watered Laban's sheep. He then entered his uncle's service, choosing Rachel as a reward for seven years of labor—years that "seemed to him like a few days because of his love" for Rachel (Gen. 29:20). Laban, we know, refusing to let Leah be stripped of the elder's birthright, secreted her within Jacob's tent on the night of his marriage. Jacob, incensed at this deceit, nonetheless completed the seven days that were his bride's due, and then demanded Rachel in exchange for seven more years of labor. During the day, he labored in the field among the flocks, and by night, he was husband to Leah and to Rachel as well as to their maids, bringing forth the twelve sons who would be Israel.

In Jacob's story, we find two key components in the fight against sloth. The first is his astonishing recognition of the presence of God. His knowledge of the Lord's presence becomes a font of creative energy which neither tires in the noonday heat nor wearies in the service of the marriage bed. Jacob's seven-year terms of labor, and the bridal week paid to Leah, recall the seven-year period of Creation in Genesis, and Jacob's fruitfulness, which overcomes and even uses Laban's deceit as a springboard to greater largesse, reminds us of the fruitfulness enjoined on Adam.

The second critical element is the manner in which time itself ceases to grip Jacob on account of the great love he has for Rachel. The desert monks afflicted by acedia, much like Achilles on the beach, much like many of us working desperately for Friday evening, are keenly aware of time's tendency to crawl by. Jacob, keyed in to God's presence and dedicated to service in love, feels that the years are as days. He is privileged with a taste of eternity, to which a thousand years are as the blinking of an eye.

Nonetheless, Jacob cannot escape the ravages of time or sin entirely. Much of the latter part of his life is fraught with the weight of his beloved Rachel's death on the road to Bethlehem. We must travel to the end of that road, to the entry of eternity into time in the Person of Christ, if we are to witness sloth's defeat. And we find guidance in our battle at the rim of Jacob's well, where Jesus encounters the Samaritan woman in John 4.

We are told that, when Jesus stopped at the well, it was about noon: the time when acedia strikes. And Jesus, like the desert monks, was hungry. He was weary with His travels. The sun hung high overhead. A woman came alone, just as Rachel had. Christ, engaging her in a sort of spiritual battle, offers her the living water that only He can give. She scoffs — surely this man cannot be greater than Jacob, who provided this well. But the Lord prevails, and the woman goes off in haste to tell everyone of this man who so intimately knows her, who has rolled the stone of sin from her heart.

The disciples return and offer Jesus the food they had procured. But He is satisfied. Doing the will of His Father has refreshed Him. And this is the food which will make us proof against sloth as well. When the noonday devil strikes, the monk's best defense is to remain in his cell, to carry on beneath the yoke of the Father's will. When sloth takes hold of us, our victory is not to be found in flight, in rushing off to do a hundred distracting tasks, but in performing the work which is set before us—playing with our children, paying our bills, laboring with our spouses, and above all giving worship to God in the Mass.

Jacob raised altars and moved the stone from the shepherds' well. Christ would be raised on the altar of the Cross at the hour of the noonday devil, and the stone would be rolled from the mouth of the tomb from which a flood of grace would well up to wash over the world. We will look in time to the Paschal Mystery as key to shaking off the sloth of our age. For now, though, we must turn to the question of why our age is so prone to this sin.

2

Acedia's Ascendancy

We are told in Genesis 3 that the serpent was the most cunning of all the creatures. Likewise, Exodus 1 portrays a Pharaoh who dealt shrewdly with Israel. The serpent disrupted the harmony of Eden, just as Pharaoh destroyed the peace Israel had known in Egypt for nearly four hundred years. The devil's shrewdness lies partly in his ability to dissect man's nature, to sow doubt and division along the joints of man's being in order to sunder him from God, from his neighbor, and from his very self. The serpent, questioning Eve about God's prohibition, relied on her own inclination toward truth, goodness, and beauty to lead her astray as he pointed out the loveliness of the fruit and its usefulness for attaining wisdom. Pharaoh crushed the fervor with which Israel first met Moses by striking at the very worship that would have made the people free.

The noonday devil, we have pointed out, is so effective, so confusing, because he does not simply turn man's attention to such subsidiary goods as honor, pleasure, or wealth, but rather makes man hate the very good to which he is naturally disposed. This hatred of our highest good has in turn caused modern man to despise the Lord's Day, the moment of eternity that is meant to make man free in the midst of the temporal procession of life.

If acedia has caused our culture to reject the Lord's Day, we ought to ask why it is that our culture is so prone to acedia. Only when the causes of acedia's prominence are recognized will we be able to address ourselves to the cure. It is one thing, by way of comparison, to recognize that a certain bacterium is causing a sickness. It is another to understand the inner workings of that bacterium and the environmental conditions in which it thrives so that we can select a remedy which disrupts its life processes and adjust the surrounding environment to discourage its recovery.

Our inquiry will consist of three parts:

1. A consideration of human nature and the elevation it experienced through the Paschal Mystery, with a particular eye to St. Thomas Aquinas's faculty psychology and St. Augustine's understanding of time;

2. A survey of the manner in which modern industrialization and the subsequent shaping of world economies has disrupted man's relationship with space and time, especially through usury;

3. A brief summary of the technological, philosophical, and sexual upheaval which has followed in the wake of this economic disruption.

On Human Nature

Acedia, by causing us to sorrow over not just the good but the divine good, strikes at our nature on a teleological level. That is, all men by nature desire the good, and especially the highest good, the one whereby we become partakers in the divine life. Acedia makes the best of all things hateful to us, stripping our nature of the drive that fundamentally orients it to its divine end.

Nature, says Aristotle, concerns those things that happen always or for the most part.[43] Thus, fire always rises and always consumes its substrate. Thus, rivers flow seaward. Thus, a well-made chair upholds the one who sits upon it. The beauty of nature which we observe in the motions of planets, the spouting of whales, the growth of forests, and the blossoming of flowers proceeds according to such teleological processes. Things work toward their ends, with those ends serving as harmonizing principles to bring each creature's various components to bear on achieving that end.

Questions arise quickly when we turn from nature, generally conceived, to human nature. That is, if whales and planets, chairs and desks, flowers and fires all have ends toward which they inherently tend, to the degree that those ends almost always come about, what are we to make of humans? What, if anything, is man's natural end?

Aristotle, continuing his analysis of nature, concludes that man, too, has a natural end, namely, happiness in contemplation of the highest things. Such contemplation, which is the closest man can draw to the eternal bliss of the unmoved mover's contemplation of himself, satisfies man not only by elevating his highest capacities to their highest possible action but also by harmonizing all of his lesser faculties in an ontological unity which frequently eludes man during his life on earth.[44]

The Church has, throughout the ages, found many forms of expression for this understanding of man's nature. The *Catechism of the Catholic Church* begins, "God, infinitely perfect and blessed in himself, in a plan of sheer goodness freely created man to make

---

[43] Aristotle, *Physics*, bk. 2, pt. 5.
[44] Aristotle, *Metaphysics*, bk. 12, pt. 7.

him share in his own blessed life" (no. 1). St. Ignatius of Loyola begins his *Exercises* thus: "Man is created to praise, reverence, and serve God our Lord, and by this means to save his soul."[45] Christ, when asked what the greatest commandment is, what the guidepost for all human activity ought to be, replies that we are to love the Lord our God with all our mind, soul, and heart (Matt. 22:37). From the beginning, God has called man to contemplative union with Him, to a sharing in the life of the Trinity, which is the fulfillment of all Sabbath rest, all Lord's Day worship, all our labors.

Though contemplative activity is man's end, Aristotle notes that we only enjoy such activity on rare occasions. The eternal bliss of the unmoved mover is something we can only approach during the loftiest moments of our lives. This raises a very curious difficulty with human nature; namely, that while nature concerns things which happen always or for the most part—like the fire's rising or the water's falling—human nature reaches its end only a small portion of the time. At least, looking at our own experience and at the apparent state of most of our fellows, moments of happiness and contemplation are few and far between.

The infrequency with which man achieves his alleged telos has led some recent philosophers, such as Jean-Paul Sartre, to claim that there is no human nature because there is no God to fashion human nature. That is, while things made by humans have purposes, those purposes derive from the human makers. For humans, though, he argues that, since we have no maker, we have no end. Such a view is one of the chief weapons in the noonday devil's arsenal, as we will see. Yet, even if we hold

---

[45] St. Ignatius of Loyola, *Spiritual Exercises*, First Principle and Foundation, trans. Fr. Elder Mullan, CCEL, https://ccel.org/ccel/ignatius/exercises/exercises.i.html.

with Aristotle in affirming that man is meant for happiness in a contemplative life akin to that enjoyed by God Himself, we nonetheless can see how sloth exploits the peculiarities of man's nature in turning him to hatred of his end. For it is our enduring experience that "man is born unto trouble, as the sparks fly upward" (Job 5:7, KJV).

Part of man's difficulty lies in his ontological makeup. Unlike a stone or a flame, a rose or a whale, man often finds himself at odds with himself. A stone reaches its end when it achieves the lowest place available to it, and its mass conduces unfailingly to that end. A dog's senses, limbs, and coat all aid it in finding nourishment and shelter and in bringing forth puppies. But man frequently finds his mind at war with his flesh, his intellectual appetites set against his physical ones, his love of God against his inclination to sin. It takes a great deal of grace and a profound habit of virtue to harmonize the several faculties of man. Even for the virtuous man, the struggle between doing the good he wishes and the evil he does not wish frequently remains intense (Rom. 7:19).

We have seen already how acedia exploits this division of human faculties. As St. Thomas explains, and as the witness of the desert monks testifies, the noonday devil launches his attack via the weariness of the body when it has endured long hours of prayer and fasting. The three hours from noon to three, the hours Christ hung upon the Cross, then become a daily proving ground wherein sloth seeks to use that bodily weariness to overthrow the mind, to induce the mind to reject the goodness of creation and of God's will for man in his specific place in that creation. The one who would overcome acedia must hang with Christ in the bodily and spiritual agony of the Cross, never allowing that agony to make him reject the goodness of God's work.

In addition to the division of faculties that sloth would exploit, man's manner of encountering reality through those faculties provides an especially deadly weapon to the enemy. For while man is called to eternal contemplation of the Triune God, he exists here on earth in time. Time, as St. Augustine describes it, is at the root of much of man's anxiety and thus of man's sin. In book 11 of his *Confessions*, Augustine calls time nothing but a distension of the mind, the triple negativity whereby the mind is continually torn apart between the no-longer of the past and the not-yet of the future, unable ever to rest in the non-extended moment of the present.[46]

Man knows all too well the anxiety which attends this experience of time. We can't stop thinking about the comment a colleague made last week, nor can we forget about the deadline tomorrow or the payment due Friday or the surgery scheduled for next month. In being drawn out of the present, we grow anxious, and we set about distracting ourselves, trying to force our attention to the present by means of television, pills, liquor, sex, sports, and all the endless variety of life which, though good in its season, may so easily work to our detriment.

Augustine goes on to point out that the way we find ourselves psychologically distended by time prevents us from preparing ourselves for our heavenly end. If Heaven is nothing other than eternal presence to the Father, our time on earth must be spent in learning to direct our attention to God, to be present to Him in recognition of the fact that He is eternally present to us. In other words, if we can never learn to rest in God's presence while in time, how will we manage to endure that presence for eternity?[47] The Lord's Day, as

[46] Augustine, *Confessions*, bk. 11.
[47] Ibid., 244.

we will consider at greater length, is a school of eternity, a moment of attention to the eternal Trinity that, properly observed, becomes a harmonizing principle for all of our temporal experience. We have seen already how sloth uses our experience of time against us. From the desert monk staring at the sun, desperate for it to move more quickly, to the modern man who feels his heart sink as the minutes of Sunday creep by en route to the beginning of another dull workweek, sloth tends to employ time to make us hate the labor to which God's will has called us and the worship that is prefatory to our ultimate heavenly rest.

Sloth strikes at man teleologically, endeavoring to make him hate the thing for which he was made. Our many faculties, drawn at once to several goods, and our capacity for experiencing time through the senses allied to memory and anticipation, supply two chief means whereby sloth may disrupt man's highest operation and so contribute to this curious fact of human nature; namely, that it so seldom seems to reach its end.

With these considerations in hand, particularly with respect to time, we turn now to two of the chief factors in the rise of modern acedia: industrialization and global reliance on usurious economies.

The Industrial World

In the pages that follow, we will deal in a general sense with the shift from a premodern (dare we say medieval) economy to a modern one. Our study must proceed with great caution, and under the caveat that we are not studying economy in the narrow sense which attends the word today. Rather, we are considering economy as a law of life, as the principle and motivation that determines man's pattern of daily life on earth. As such, our interest is not primarily with what could be called a scientific study of socioeconomic trends in the last few centuries but more so, given man's psychological makeup and its temporal orientation, with what effect industry, usury, science, and technology, as they have developed in modernity, have had on man's disposition toward God, nature, and himself.

We may identify three broad shifts that have defined the transition from a premodern economy to a modern one. (No doubt other trends exist, but the three at hand are most critical for our present study of acedia and the Lord's Day.)

First, we see a dramatic shift in America from rural to urban living. In 1800, 94 percent of Americans lived in rural settings. By 1990, just a quarter of Americans lived in the country, with 75 percent occupying urban areas. By 2020, that figure had risen to 80 percent.[48] The trend is not simply American, of course. At present, over 55 percent of the world's population lives in urban areas, with that number expected to grow to roughly 65 percent by 2050.[49]

The shift toward the cities has likewise seen the majority of Americans moving away from agricultural labor toward work in manufacturing, construction, and commerce. In 1800, 83 percent of Americans worked in agriculture. Today, agricultural interests represent 10.3 percent of American labor.[50]

Third, across all sectors of life—rural or urban, agricultural or industrial—America has become vastly more technological. It is

---

[48] "Nation's Urban and Rural Populations Shift Following 2020 Census," United States Census Bureau, December 29, 2022, https://www.census.gov/newsroom/press-releases/2022/urban-rural-populations.html.

[49] "Overview" of Urban Development, World Bank, April 3, 2023, https://www.worldbank.org/en/topic/urbandevelopment/overview.

[50] S. Mintz and S. McNeil, "Agriculture," Digital History, accessed December 6, 2023, https://www.digitalhistory.uh.edu/disp_textbook.cfm?smtID=11&psid=3837.

by some standards fair to say that man's experience of the world changed more between A.D. 1900 and 2000 than it did between 800 B.C. and A.D. 1900. A century of automobiles, washing machines, airplanes, moon landings, nuclear weapons, deep space telescopes, laptops, chemotherapy, televisions, and air conditioners has created a world that could well seem far stranger to Abraham Lincoln than Lincoln's world would have to Homer.

To these three trends we could append three general effects on man and his relationship to the cosmos and its Creator. These are tendencies first, to reduce man to his material aspect; second, to make work itself seem a curse; and third, to inhibit man's ability to worship.

The evils of industrialism are well known. The portrayals of their piteousness in the works of Dickens, Blake, and Sinclair have ingrained themselves in our cultural imagination, and Hilaire Belloc also wrote freely of the "poisonous effects of Industrialization."[51] Such industrialization, he noted, had as its sole goal the accumulation of material wealth. The Catholic Land Movement associated with Belloc has spoken in unequivocal terms of that poison: "Industrialism centralized production and thereby created a monopolistic economy under which millions of people had been forced (or seduced) from farm and village, to take up a barrack-like existence in burgeoning cities. The loss of property subsequently reduced most Englishmen to a state of economic servility."[52]

It could be supposed, however, and is clear in the list of twentieth-century innovations noted above, that the shift toward

---

[51] Hilaire Belloc, preface, in John McQuillan et al., *Flee to the Fields: The Faith and Works of the Catholic Land Movement* (London: Heath Cranton, 1934), 15.

[52] Tobias Lanz, "Introduction," in McQuillan, *Flee to the Fields*, 7.

mechanism is not inherently evil, nor have the results of these innovations been all bad. Belloc himself noted that what "has made industrial capitalism is not the machine but the mind of man perverted by a false philosophy."[53] However much we might like the image of the bucolic past, we must recall that the rural, agricultural world of yesteryear, even the medieval world of St. Thomas Aquinas, was nonetheless a fallen world. And however different London and Athens look today from how they did in 1588 or 350 B.C., the human heart known to Shakespeare and to Aristotle looks more or less the same as it has since Adam fell. It will look much the same when the last trumpet sounds. The character of the human heart notwithstanding, modernity has brought with it immense advances in man's ability to know the universe, to rejoice in God's creative design, and to rest in contemplation of divine love—provided he has the prudence and fortitude to do so.[54]

Our interest is not, then, in whether modernity is in itself better or worse than the medieval or premodern world. Rather, we wish to ask if there are ways in which the modern manner of living contributes to the power of acedia and thus to the decline in observance of the Lord's Day. Put otherwise, our question is this: How do the lineaments of modern life tend to distract man from God's presence and ultimately make that presence odious?

The Insular City

One of the chief trends in modern life is from the rural to the urban setting. We must note, of course, that the city itself is not a strictly modern development. Cities have always marked civilization, from

---

[53] Belloc, "Preface," 16.
[54] See John Paul II, Encyclical Letter *Redemptor Hominis* (March 4, 1979), no. 16.

Troy to Athens, from Rome to Paris, from London to New York. Cities afford opportunities for the development of such advanced culture as can hardly be achieved by isolated families living in the country. A well-ordered city becomes a locus of *urbanitas*, that spirit of cultural flourishing which allows for the exaltation of the human spirit reaching out joyfully to God.[55] Without the city, we would have no Plato, no Augustine, no Aquinas, no Lemaître. We would have no Chartres Cathedral or Florentine Duomo, no *Divine Comedy* or *Odyssey*, no *Ode to Joy* or *Clarinet Concerto*.

Even for those who live in a rural, agricultural setting, the city plays an important role as the locus of exchange, center of religious life, and resort in case of sickness, crop failure, or natural disaster. Even the most assiduous farmer stands to benefit from a community with which he can trade, and certainly his sacramental life depends on his proximity to a parish.

Nonetheless, as Fr. Vincent McNabb observes, we may make the general distinction that while people move from the land to the city for material ends, they move from the city to the land in pursuit of true worship.[56] This, at least, is the paradigm established by Israel's going down to Egypt and being led forth again. They went to Egypt in a time of famine; they were blessed there, enjoying the material abundance that transformed them from a tribe into a nation. Yet, in order to learn true worship, they had to go out from the city, into the desert, away from the fruit and the fleshpots and the great works of urban man to the lean and star-filled simplicity of the desert.

[55] Romano Guardini, *Letters from Lake Como: Explorations in Technology and the Human Race*, trans. Geoffrey W. Bromiley (Grand Rapids, MI: W. B. Eerdmans, 1994), 6–7.

[56] Fr. Vincent McNabb, "A Call to Contemplatives," in *The Church and the Land* (Norfolk, VA: IHS Press, 2003), 31–34.

The shift from rural to urban living witnessed by the modern world has served in general to deaden man's sensibility to the rhythms of nature. Such rhythms provide built-in seasons of productivity and rest, of labor and festivity, of seeding and harvesting and storing away. As he goes from his air-conditioned home to his air-conditioned car to his air-conditioned office and back again, modern man can afford more or less to ignore the conditions of the outside world. Every day of the year, he finds the supermarket shelves laden with the same squash, zucchini, strawberries, kale, peaches, and pineapples. Seasonal climate change means little to him. Whether in July or December, he goes to work five days a week and performs the same tasks year after year.

Again, we should not present these advances beyond absolute dependence on weather and climate as somehow unequivocally evil. What a comfort it is to a parent to have the means to shield his children against the winter's cold or to feed them apples and pears and all manner of nourishing food. Agricultural and technological progress may be perfectly consonant with man's call to fill the earth and subdue it, cultivating it according to the power of his mind.

The dangers in these advances, however, and the means by which they render us more prone to acedia and rejection of the Lord's Day, are two. In the first place, the capacity to insulate ourselves against the fluctuations of the natural world may well lead us to forget our fundamental dependence on God or, perhaps, in the spirit of Babel, to attempt to raise ourselves to the level of gods. When a man of sufficient means surveys the world about him, it is easy for him to act as though his security is inviolable, like the rich man of the parable who built larger barns to house his great surplus, only to have his life demanded of him that very night (Luke 12:16–21). The modern world seeks in many ways to render all of us such rich men, proof against all acts of God, man, or nature.

Second, and very closely connected to this propensity toward forgetfulness of God, is the possibility that modern life, isolated from the rhythms of the natural world, can create of man's existence a kind of false horizontal infinity, an unending procession of workweeks trudging on toward a bleary retirement and a morphine-dulled death. Day follows day, week follows week, and we perform the same labors again and again without any Sabbath refreshment or festival retreat. Such false infinites are always present in human life, as Hegel points out in his discussion of appetites, which follow upon each other in endless succession from birth till death, or in the apparently limitless variety of finite bodies the human soul may take.[57] The danger lies in the possibility of life itself becoming such a succession, devoid of any transcendent awareness of the eternal God who underlies all temporal change. In falling victim to this attitude, we forget the possibility of worship, of attending for a moment to that which lies beyond all succession of time—or, worse still, such worship becomes hateful to us, an interruption of our labor in moving on steadily toward death.

The End of Agriculture

Similar dangers lie in the transition away from a predominantly agricultural economy. Here again, we do not wish to conjure images of a bucolic past for which those of us trapped in the digital age can only raise pitiful laments. An agricultural existence, as people since Adam and Cain have known, demands a life of often backbreaking labor. The exigencies of weather, insects, and blight

---

[57] Hegel, *Philosophy of Mind*, trans. W. Wallace and A. V. Miller (Oxford: Oxford University Press, 2010), 50.

can all occasion that intense temporal anxiety St. Augustine described. And a poorly managed farm, as anyone who has driven many southern back roads knows, can be every bit as aesthetically offensive as a city.

Nonetheless, those who live according to the rhythms of the land necessarily encounter something of the natural order of creation, an order which includes moments of frantic seminal labor as well as moments of repose. In her book *The Passion of the Infant Christ*, Carryl Houselander reflects on the fitness of Christ's having come into the world—and of our observing that advent—at the time of the year when things lie fallow. Winter, where agriculture is concerned, is often a time of some measure of rest, a time of reflecting on and enjoying the fruits of the autumn harvest, and a time of laying sound plans for the crops to be seeded when the soil begins to soften in spring. That time is ideal for contemplating the mystery of Christ's reception in time. Houselander's book begins with a lovely passage describing the kind of peace that attends good labor: "The countryman is not impatient because the season of flowers and fruit is swiftly over and the winter is so long. He comes in early from his fields, to doze content while firelight weaves the long dusk with gold.... He has lived through cruel winters ... but he knows that with spring the snowdrop comes again ... that the life that is in all living things is stronger than death. That is the knowledge which is the root of his peace."[58]

In short, the true laborer in the field, because he feels the rhythm of all life in the rhythm of his land, comes to see time not as an occasion for anxiety. The labors to come and the storms behind do not worry him. Rather, he has peace in the sure knowledge

---

[58] Caryll Houselander, *The Passion of the Infant Christ* (New York: Sheed and Ward, 1949), 1.

that time is the river of God's grace. He learns, as Hans Urs von Balthasar puts it, that "Time is the school of exuberance, the school of magnanimity ... the grand school of love."[59]

Again, as Houselander intuits, this knowledge proceeds from living according to the rhythms of nature: "The man who grows wheat, who ploughs and sows and reaps, who sets his pace to the rhythm and time of cycles of light, to seasons of gestation and birth, death and resurrection; who measures by the shadows of the sun and calculates by the width of the skies, lives, even if he does not fully realize it, in harmony with the Eternal Law of Love."[60]

Such rhythm often eludes the urban man, the man of the office, of the assembly line, of the computer screen and the smartphone. The temperature is the same in the office and in the car and at home. The light is even at work and in the apartment. He exists, in the particularly populous cities, within a series of anti-monkish cells, with the space between a realm of terror,[61] not because of demons or desert beasts, but because of his fellow men, moving frightened and transparent through the ashen, sulfurous air.

Technology

The transition to a modern mechanical and technological idiom has further accentuated the horizontal orientation of human life, which isolates man from the rhythms of nature and disrupts his natural inclination to transcendence. Modern labor tends to revolve around the repetition of tasks that have little connection to the order of nature or, from a laborer's perspective, to the order of

[59] Balthasar, *Heart of the World*, 25.
[60] Houselander, *Passion of the Infant Christ*, 5.
[61] Walker Percy, "New Orleans mon Amour," in *Signposts in a Strange Land*, 10ff.

production in general. A cashier scans the same items ad infinitum, with many items costing more than his hourly wage pays him. A stocker fills the shelves, watches them empty out, and fills them again. The line of customers rolls on and on, and the burgers and fries are wrapped and bagged and handed out the window to be devoured on the way to the office, where the same reports will be prepared, the same e-mails sent, the same forms filed. Even the farmer of today, relying heavily on tractors, combine harvesters, and industrial chicken houses, has become more and more an apparatus of the technological engine of modern living, and his labor may thus become more decidedly monotonous. We are awash in sameness, to the degree that, as Walker Percy says, the question is not so much "What do we do if the bomb drops?" as "What do we do if it does not?" How do we go about the work of getting through an ordinary Wednesday afternoon?[62] We watch the news and pray for some disaster to disrupt the mechanical rut into which we have wandered.

Of course, any work can be done joyfully and well. All work, as St. John Paul II pointed out in *Laborem Exercens*, takes its dignity from the human subject who performs it.[63] The humblest and most mundane of tasks is thus transformed through the dignity of the human person created through God's love. And if there is some pain in much of our labor, even when we labor in the awareness of divine charity, we can attribute some measure of this to the burden of sin. At the same time, the very dignity of the person makes it possible that his or her work, viewed as somehow separate

---

[62] Walker Percy, *The Message in the Bottle: How Queer Man Is, How Queer Language Is, and What One Has to Do with the Other* (New York: Farrar, Straus, and Giroux, 1975), 84–85.

[63] John Paul II, Encyclical Letter on Human Labor *Laborem Exercens* (September 14, 1981), no. 6.

from the working of God's will in the world, can come to seem eminently odious. And there appear to be many instances of such odium in our age.

How has this change come about? In the first place, it bears repeating that the malaise arising from modern forms of industry is not entirely restricted to the modern world. The farmer and the textile manufacturer and the painter of the Middle Ages also had to put up with such mind-numbing labor as seeding acre after acre of earth or running a needle through a million stitches or executing a big order of family portraits in order to get by. But he also had the satisfaction of watching the fallow earth rise up in ears of wheat, of bringing to the market now flour, now fowl, now beef. He watched the single stitch become a shirt, a gown, or a coat. He knew the wonder of turning his eyes on a human face and seeing it more truly than his fellow man or even a modern camera can see.[64]

Our inquiry into this shift to the mechanical milieu and its alliance with acedia will be aided by an understanding of the distinction between the premodern concept of *techne* and the modern concept of the technological. For the ancients, as well as for the medievals, all arts — the mechanical as well as the fine — were gathered up in the term *techne*, which essentially means craft.[65] A farmer and a potter, a farrier and a shipbuilder, a dramatist and a sculptor were all men of *techne*. A fundamental characteristic of techne, as Martin Heidegger points out, is that it works in harmony with nature to achieve its end. A carpenter does not choose wood

---

[64] Caldecott, *Not as the World Gives*, 160.

[65] Jacques Maritain, *Art and Scholasticism and the Frontiers of Poetry*, trans. Joseph W. Evans (Notre Dame: University of Notre Dame Press, 1974), 8-9.

at random in order to beat it into submission in framing a house or fashioning a chair. Rather, he chooses such wood as will best suit his project—cedar or juniper for a raised garden bed, for instance, and oak or mahogany for a desk. A bridge builder does not see a river as an obstacle to be dominated but rather as a feature of a landscape to which he adds his own pleasing accent. A poet does not force human nature into the shape he desires but rather holds a mirror up to nature, even as he uses that mirror to shine light here or to cast shadow there, refining nature through the intellect.

Such are the lineaments of a culture that encounters nature via techne, through authentic craft. A culture that is technological, Heidegger says, seeks rather to "enframe" nature so as to make of it a standing reserve, a resource which may be tapped at will, typically for political or financial ends.[66]

Consider a dam. Rather than a bridge, which, as it were, steps through the river, respecting its integrity while affording passage over its loveliness and its power, a dam turns a river into a standing reserve, whether of electrical power, of water reserves, or both. In flooding valleys and turning forests into reservoirs, a dam fundamentally alters the landscape it taps.

The effects here need not be all bad. The use of technology to create stable environments where culture can flourish can quite reasonably be squared with man's commission to subdue the earth. Indeed, the results are often quite beautiful, as for instance in the many lovely reservoirs of Arkansas, where reliable water supplies serve also as homes to innumerable fish and other wildlife and

---

[66] Martin Heidegger, "The Question Concerning Technology," in *Basic Writings: From* Being and Time *(1927) to* The Task of Thinking *(1964)*, ed. David Farrell Krell (New York: Harper and Row, 1977), 321ff.

as spaces where man can enjoy authentic recreation against the backdrop of the natural world.

Yet there remains the danger that man might abuse the natural world and himself. Irresponsible mining, forestry, and agricultural techniques denude the landscapes and denigrate the men who labor amid them. The frightening possibility Heidegger envisions is one in which man himself becomes the standing reserve which can be drawn upon at the will of the corporation or the tyrant in pursuit of his ends.

Indeed, Stratford Caldecott suggests that in the technological—and Heidegger is approaching the same point via his distinction between techne and the technological—we find not merely a morally neutral set of tools to be used for good or evil according to the will of the user, but rather a fundamental attitude toward man and nature.[67] In the use of child or slave labor, for instance, man becomes a mere means to the end of the cheapest possible production and the highest possible profit. More globally, though more insidiously, modern technology provides for the division of mankind into consumerist aggregates serving as a reliable, malleable profit base.

Over the last decade, Apple has offered a master class in the development of just such a human standing reserve. Its status as one of the world's most profitable companies rests heavily on the success of the iPhone. And the iPhone has performed so well largely due to the company's method of delivery, wherein the purchase of the device is typically tethered to a two-year contract with a wireless service provider. The brilliance of the scheme lies partly in its ability to ease consumer anxiety at rising price tags by spreading actual cost ($499 for the original iPhone, with high-end models

---

[67] Caldecott, *Not as the World Gives*, 92.

now running in excess of $1,000) over twenty-four low, monthly payments. The logic is the car dealer's: Go ahead, get the new one! Your monthly payment's staying the same! The scheme works wonders. America alone is home to some 113 million iPhone users, while globally the sleek devices grace the hands of more than a billion. And the majority of iPhone users in the United States upgrade as soon as their wireless provider contracts allow. All told, the tech giant can count on Americans to buy something like 200 million iPhones annually.[68]

Already we can see some of the ways in which such technological enframing contributes to acedia's rise. The psychology of such consumerism is almost entirely horizontal. The concern is no longer with the real cost of the iPhone, let alone with its compatibility with man's telos, but rather with its compatibility with the monthly budget. The eye is trained to look forward to the release of next year's model, and a subtle anxiety creeps in that we will be left behind with the Luddite crew, still sporting five-year-old devices. All through the day, at the faintest hint of distaste at the work set before us, at the paperwork to be filed or the dishes to be washed or the children to be bathed, we turn to our phones for the cold, backlit comfort of distraction. All during Mass, we feel vibrations in our pockets and wonder through the Gospel and the Consecration who might be calling or texting. As we read through the Liturgy of the Hours on our breviary apps, messages and notifications flash across the tops of our screens, beckoning us away from prayer. And, as we try to eat our Sunday dinners with our families, e-mails from customers and bosses trickle in, often demanding answers in minutes.

[68] David Curry, "Apple Statistics (2023)," Business of Apps, November 6, 2023, https://www.businessofapps.com/data/apple-statistics/.

Technology makes man a standing reserve, not simply by inur-
ing him to a cycle of product consumption, but also by making
him constantly available. His attention is at every moment subject
to the demands of his boss, to the commentary of his social-media
contacts, to the exigencies of the weather, to the harking of the
news, to the suggestions of the advertisers. Through its apps and
widgets, his phone makes him a reserve for a vast network of corporations, politicians, and influencers, all vying for the presence
man owes to God.

Technology thus creates, in addition to the temporal distension
St. Augustine saw at the heart of man's sinful anxiety, a kind of
spatial distension. No longer is man simply taken out of the present
moment by worries about the past and the future so that he fails to
attend to God. His attention is also distended in space. News and
social media draw him away from his family, his friends, his work,
and those other concrete elements of life which express the divine
will in each moment. Thus, he is worried not only about happen-
ings yesterday and tomorrow but also about those in Myanmar,
Iran, and Burkina Faso. In view of the war on a far continent, the
genocide far to the south, and the pandemic sweeping over the
earth, the daily concerns of life and the actual labors set before
us come to seem insubstantial; like the desert monks of old, we
grow to hate our own place and time. As Wendell Berry has put
it, the modern relation to space and time may be characterized as
"withhold[ing] ourselves from the present, and from everything
that is present with us: our families, our neighbors, our places."[69]

An especially fine example of the difference between techne
in the classical sense and technology in the modern, industrial

[69] Wendell Berry, *The Art of Loading Brush: New Agrarian Writings*
(Berkeley, CA: Counterpoint, 2017), 101.

sense may be found in the present effort to restore Paris's Notre Dame Cathedral. The fire, which raged there in April of 2019, devastated the roof structure, known as *La Forêt* (the forest) for the immense number of timbers used in its construction. Many said that reconstruction according to the original plan, which took more than a century's skilled labor, would be impossible. Yet a group of craftsmen at Guedélon Castle in Burgundy have rediscovered the art of medieval carpentry, and many of the firms seeking to undertake the cathedral's restoration have come to Guedélon to engage the carpenters' services. Stephane Boudy, who has worked at Guedélon since 1999, explains how "hand-hewing each beam—a single piece from a single tree—respects the 'heart' of the green wood that gives it its strength and resistance." According to Boudy, it is this sort of labor, the kind that works according to the nature of the wood itself, that has given Notre Dame its extraordinary longevity. As he says, "If Notre Dame's roof lasted 800 years, it is because of this. There's no heart in sawmill wood."[70] The sawmill aims primarily at profit, and it uses the means most suitable to that end. The true craftsman aims at excellence. His labor lasts longer, and the results last longer as well.

In extreme cases, the power of technology may become so great that much more than the longevity of construction begins to be at stake. As St. John Paul II pointed out in his first encyclical, man's creations may come so effectively to dominate him that his very existence is threatened.[71] Especially when technology is allied to the machinations of despots, millions on millions of men may

---

[70] Kim Willsher, "'They Said It Was Impossible': How Medieval Carpenters Are Rebuilding Notre Dame," *The Guardian*, August 20, 2022.

[71] John Paul II, *Redemptor Hominis*, no. 16.

be reduced to mere slave labor, as in Pharaoh's Egypt or Stalin's Russia, or they may simply be used as casualties of war, slaughtered to force an enemy's hand. Not all technology does this, John Paul affirms, nor even does most of it. But the worst of it has played a key role in ushering in the culture of death that seeks at every turn to prevent man from lifting his mind to his Creator, that distracts him, heaps labor upon him, and would even kill him if only to stop him from offering worship.

The most dangerous of these industrial trends toward the cities, away from nature, and into the hands of technology are allied, as Belloc and others have noted, to greed; with this in mind, we turn now to consider a key arrow in the quiver of sloth: usury.

Usury

For a long time now, America has been embroiled in argument over the cost of education. Debates over the practicability or the necessity of student debt forgiveness have become especially intense in recent years. Some citizens have rejoiced at the prospect of such forgiveness; others have decried it as the epitome of a kind of craven charity trotted out to buy power. Curiously, among those in support of forgiveness, or at least of broad educational finance reform, there have arisen many cries reminding us of the evil of usury. The outrageous cost of education, coupled with unconscionable interest rates, has left many borrowers to repay the amount of their initial loans many times over. Some online commentators have taken this as an opportunity to remind the world that, in the eyes of the Catholic Church, usury remains a sin.

Otherwise, however, lending and borrowing at interest have become so much a part of life that we rarely give the matter much thought. C. S. Lewis observes something of the fundamental economic shift in modern life in *Mere Christianity*: "There is one bit of advice given to us by the ancient heathen Greeks, and by the Jews in the Old Testament, and by the great Christian teachers of the Middle Ages, which the modern economic system has completely disobeyed. All these people told us not to lend money at interest: and lending money at interest—what we call investment—is the basis of our whole system."[72]

This is, as Lewis goes on to say, more or less mere observation. Financial customs, like fashions in cuisine or dress or even to some degree aesthetics, may admit of a range of ethically viable options. As Lewis continues, "It may not absolutely follow that we are wrong. Some people say that when Moses and Aristotle and the Christians agreed in forbidding interest (or 'usury' as they called it), they could not foresee the joint stock company, and were only thinking of the private moneylender, and that, therefore, we need not bother about what they said."[73]

Lewis is not alone in mentioning the issue. The drama of John Steinbeck's *The Grapes of Wrath* hinges heavily on the disjunct which exists between man and the American landscape as a result of mortgages on farms and installment loans on heavy machinery. Classic American stories such as Washington Irving's "The Devil and Tom Walker" make usury one of the devil's preferred schemes. And Ezra Pound's poem "With Usura" tethers lending at interest to everything from poor craftsmanship to broken marriages to abortion.

Nor is such criticism limited to the poets. Pope Leo XIII notes in *Rerum Novarum*: "Working men have been surrendered, isolated and helpless, to the hardheartedness of employers and the greed

---

[72] C. S. Lewis, *Mere Christianity* (New York: Collier Books, 1952), 80–81.
[73] Ibid.

of unchecked competition. The mischief has been increased by rapacious usury, which, although more than once condemned by the Church, is nevertheless, under a different guise, but with like injustice, still practiced by covetous and grasping men."[74]

Indeed, the interest of capital proves so overpowering that, in many cases, as Leo XIII noted, and as Pope John Paul II echoed, it threatens man's very ability to worship by denying him the freedom to worship—the selfsame freedom that was also denied him by Pharaoh.[75]

What, then, is usury, and how has it come to form part of the fabric of our world? First, we will briefly consider what Scripture says on the matter. Then we shall turn to the Church Fathers and to the medievals, particularly St. Thomas Aquinas. We will conclude our sketch with a glimpse of the modern Church's stance with regard to usury. To be clear, though, our concern here is not primarily with economy in a strict financial sense. Rather, we want to understand how usury, especially as it manifests in the modern world, affects man on a psychological level. How does it exacerbate man's tendency to be drawn out of the present and away from attention to God? How does it incline him to the attacks of acedia? And, most of all, how does it draw him away from Lord's Day worship?

Usury, in Brief

The Old Testament is filled with injunctions against lending money at interest. "If you lend money to my people, the poor among you,

---

[74] Pope Leo XIII, Encyclical Letter on Capital and Labor *Rerum Novarum* (May 15, 1891), no. 3.

[75] See Pope Leo XIII, *Rerum Novarum*; and Pope John Paul II, Encyclical Letter on the Hundredth Anniversary of *Rerum Novarum*, *Centesimus Annus* (May 1, 1991), no. 9.

you must not be like a money lender; you must not demand interest from them" (Exod. 22:24). "Do not give your money at interest or your food at a profit" (Lev. 25:37). "A son who … lends at interest and exacts usury—this son certainly shall not live" (Ezek. 18:11–13).

Such prohibitions abound. While some of them seem indeed to forbid lending at interest in general, it must be noted that these injunctions aim to protect the Israelites and are especially solicitous of the poor. The passage from Exodus quoted above, for example, specifies the attitude an Israelite must have in dealing with a poor brother or sister. Likewise, the passage from Leviticus, taken from a longer section concerning the Jubilee years which would bring remission of economic burdens, manifests God's care for the poor and downtrodden among His people.

Other texts go on to accent some of the nuances in Old Testament monetary policy. Deuteronomy 23:21 specifies, "From a foreigner you may demand interest, but you may not demand interest from your kindred, so that the LORD, your God, may bless you in all your undertakings on the land you are to enter and possess." The covenantal bond, whereby God and the people have been made one through the sprinkling of a bull's blood at Sinai, demands that even the contractual obligations of the people be tempered at every turn by a remembrance of the incomparable greatness of the Lord who has redeemed His people. Just as each man has received his very being from the Lord, without possibility of repayment, so should he lend freely to his neighbor, acting as a secondary cause in extending being to the world around him.

The New Testament, less explicit than the Old where usury is concerned, follows its covenantal logic in treating of money. Christ's teaching demonstrates a preference for protection of the poor and with it a defense of the heart against the allure of riches. Christ warns His followers frequently of the division of heart which follows on money: "You cannot serve God and mammon" (Matt. 6:24); "It is easier for a camel to pass through the eye of a needle than for one who is rich to enter the kingdom of God" (Matt. 19:24); "Go, sell what you have and give to [the] poor, and you will have treasure in heaven" (Matt. 19:21).

Though Christ Himself makes no prescriptions against usury of the sort found in the Mosaic books, He does adjure us to give without expectation of repayment. Luke 6:35 became the definitive text in later ecclesial admonitions against usury: "Love your enemies and do good to them, and lend expecting nothing back; then your reward will be great and you will be children of the Most High, for he himself is kind to the ungrateful and the wicked." A modern reader tends, perhaps, to pass over the injunction to lend expecting nothing back, or to interpret it as an elaboration of Jesus' general theme here; namely, the liberality man should practice in recognition of the incomparable liberality of God in His creative and redemptive goodness. We should give freely to others as God has given freely to us. For the medieval commentators, though, this became a literal command to eschew lending at interest.

However, just as the Old Testament admitted interest in some cases, as with the foreigner, so does Jesus recognize the value of prudent investment. In the parable of the talents, for instance, the master demands to know why the servant given one talent did not at least deposit it in a bank and return the principal with interest. What is critical is not so much the interest itself, but whether interest is the result of prudential action resulting in natural increase in value or is rather directed to amassing value through predation of the poor.

The Church Fathers condemn usury, and while many of their writings on the subject are cast in such language as could be interpreted to decry all lending at interest, the force of their arguments derives chiefly from consideration for the poor. St. Jerome, for example, with Cato and Seneca, goes so far as to class the usurer with the murderer, on the grounds that the one who exacts injurious interest from a debtor sucks his very life away.[76]

St. Thomas Aquinas, ever phlegmatic, casts his argument against usury in terms of justice, on the grounds that any consumable good can only be sold for its own use and not for the use in addition to itself. It is unjust, for instance, to sell a man a bottle of wine and also sell him the right to drink that wine, which right I have of course ceded with the bottle itself. Likewise, when I lend money, I can only equitably receive back the same amount of money. St. Thomas shies away even from the idea that an investment in a business venture or the like merits a return at interest, for the reason that a businessman, who may be prevented by any number of circumstances from realizing that capitalization he foresees, has no right to contract the sale of that capitalization in advance.[77]

Now, as many have pointed out, circumstances have changed a great deal since the 1260s. Through the advent of the joint-stock company mentioned by Lewis, a great deal of risk in business investment has been mitigated. Indeed, it had been so ameliorated by the mid-eighteenth century that, as John Noonan notes, "By 1750 . . . the scholastic theory and the countertheory . . . agree in approving the common practice [of demanding interest on loans]."[78]

We thus arrive at something like the modern economy, founded almost entirely on investment, a landscape in which it is almost

---

[76] See Arthur Vermeersch, "Usury," *Catholic Encyclopedia*, vol. 15 (New York: Robert Appleton, 1912), https://www.newadvent. org/cathen/15235c.htm.

[77] St. Thomas Aquinas, *Summa Theologica* II-II, q. 78.

[78] John Thomas Noonan, *The Scholastic Analysis of Usury* (Cambridge, MA: Harvard University Press, 1957), 377.

impossible to follow Polonius's famous counsel to Laertes: "Neither a borrower nor a lender be."[79] Mortgages, car debts, student loans, and credit card accounts are balanced throughout adult life against the Roth IRA, the HSA, the ESA, and the 401(k) as working life races on toward either retirement or death.

If it is true that the ancient and medieval world's polemics against usury hinged on concern for the poor, and if it is also true that modern economic policy has created systems in which lending at interest has a very high potential to create mutually profitable financial relationships, it is nonetheless still the case that the love of money is the root of all evil. The modern economy, relatively stable as it may be, has persisted in producing means for a small minority of men to amass great wealth while a vast swath of mankind grinds on in oppressive poverty. Moreover, we propose that the modern lending system has contributed greatly to acedia's rise and the downfall of worship, and that it has done so chiefly by preying on man's tendency to be drawn apart in time, taken out of the present where God's will would encounter him.

Consider a few statistics. The average American has slightly upward of $90,000 in total debt.[80] The average American makes just over $31,000 annually. And the average American's savings account balance is just under $5,000. True, it is unfair to collate the figures thus, representing as they do a highly various set of measures. The figures suggest something of the discomfort of the system, but the very fact of their consistency over a fairly large span of time indicates that, for most people at least, such a system is more or less workable.

[79] Shakespeare, *Hamlet*, 1.3.
[80] All statistics in this paragraph come from Chris Horymski, "Experian Study: U.S. Consumer Debt Reaches $16.84 Trillion in Q2 2023," Experian Research, October 24, 2023, https://www.experian.com/blogs/ask-experian/research/consumer-debt-study/.

Most households can get by with a $200,000 mortgage spread over thirty years, a pair of auto loans traded in every few years, and a revolving balance of $5,300 on the credit cards. The question, where acedia and the Lord's Day are concerned, though, is not whether the system is viable, but whether it directs man to love his end and urges him on toward it. In general, it fails to do so because, as Leo XIII noted, it reduces man to his material dimension. It reduces life to its horizontal element, drawing man's attention out between the past and future and placing his security in money rather than in God.

For our purposes, we should consider usury under two aspects: first, ~~that form of rapacious lending that especially oppresses the poor; and second, that system of borrowing and investing that makes the average man and perhaps especially the rich man forgetful of his end.~~

It need hardly be stated that the modern system of credit and investment is skewed against the poor. If the poor are often impoverished through imprudence or other failures of virtue, they are no less poor for it, and modern society could stand to do much better by them — not, perhaps, by governmental schemes but by the generosity of citizens. In any case, if usury in the sense of excessive interest can be said to be alive and well anywhere in the modern economy, it is most of all so in the world of lending to the poor.

The current state of auto loan practices is especially illuminating in this regard. The average interest rate for subprime auto loans stands at present just over 17 percent, with rates sometimes soaring as high as 25 percent.[81] For the customer with poor credit,

---

[81] David Low, "Comparing Auto Loans for Borrowers with Subprime Credit Scores," Consumer Financial Protection Bureau, September 30, 2021, https://www.consumerfinance.gov/about-us/blog/comparing-auto-loans-borrowers-with-subprime-credit-scores/.

the results of taking out such a loan are often crippling. (Again, we may leave aside the question of what landed the customer in the situation to begin with, or whether signing to such a loan is advisable, or if it is perhaps necessary, given the layout of most American cities. We want simply to see the effect such a state of affairs has on the borrower's soul.)

Imagine a customer who needs a car to get to work and back. His credit is poor, and he has just enough money to cover his own sales tax. Based on his credit, a dealer tells him that only three vehicles on the lot will suit him. He buys a pre-owned 2018 Nissan Altima for $18,000, financing it for 72 months at a rate of 17 percent, with a monthly payment of $400.43. Assuming the car is perfect and his luck is excellent, our buyer will make his last payment in the year 2028, having paid $28,831 for an $18,000 car. Assuming such perfection, we could well argue, in defense of our usurer, that things have worked out well for everyone. It was a risk to lend the money in the first place, and the lender has been compensated for the risk. The borrower now owns a car outright, and his credit has presumably improved so that he can buy at much greater advantage.

Let's say, however, that things don't all go right. Our borrower makes two years of faithful payments, has his oil changed regularly, and drives cautiously. In those two years, he will have paid $9,600 toward his loan, but less than half of that will have gone toward the principal. Meanwhile, the value of the car will have fallen substantially. Then, most critically, the transmission fails. There is no warranty, and our borrower will have no funds to make the repairs. He has two options: either to stop making the payments and let the car be repossessed, or to trade the vehicle. The problem is that it's now a six-year-old vehicle with a bad transmission. He goes back to the dealer who sold him the car. The management team there is entirely different, though exactly the same in their desire for profit. They offer him $5,000 for the car—a generous bid, given the mechanical failure. However, he owes almost $14,000 on it still. No problem. His credit has improved, and the dealer can put him in a brand-new car that can hold the value of his negative equity. He signs a new loan for $39,000 on a new Altima. His payment will only go up to $683.80, as he now qualifies for an 8 percent interest rate.

Such a system, unless the borrower be extraordinarily lucky, holds up a target of financial freedom which continues to recede into the future. The hope of the poor in the modern world lies there, in the future, and acedia delights in this condition, urging us to dwell on the mistakes that led us to this miserable pass and on the despairing possibility of an eventual freedom which we suspect in our heart of hearts will never arrive. Then, too, the only option for many afflicted by such a system is to find more work. If that means working on Sunday, then the possibility of true rest in the Lord has fallen as well.

It is not just the poor who suffer, though. Even those who enjoy very high standards of living frequently fall prey to the same compression of human existence to the horizontal. Some two-thirds of Americans live paycheck to paycheck, and in the last six months, roughly one-third have spent more than they've earned.[82] In such a system, the pressure always mounts to become our own pharaohs, to heap more and more hours, gigs, and side hustles upon ourselves to make ends meet or to finally advance beyond the

---

[82] Tristan Bove, "Inflation is Forcing More Americans to Live Paycheck to Paycheck—Including Half of People Who Make over $100,000 a Year," *Fortune*, October 25, 2022, https://fortune .com/2022/10/25/inflation-outpaces-wage-growth-two-thirds -employed-americans-live-paycheck-to-paycheck-study/amp/.

stage of merely making ends meet. As the noonday demon makes us busier and busier, true worship ceases to delight and becomes a mere obligation before at last it falls entirely by the wayside.

Again, the danger is great, perhaps the greatest of all, for those who have gone beyond month-to-month living and attained to true financial security. The man who can buy whatever he needs may be most tempted of all to ask what need he has of God. Why worship when he can simply build bigger barns, laying up a store that will ensure his own livelihood for many lifetimes? Why close up shop on Sundays and forfeit a day's profit?

What is becoming clearer is that it is not lending and investment in themselves that are inclined to acedia and the abnegation of worship. Rather, the use of this economic system, this law of life, in the service of financial gain as the chief end of life, is the trouble. It is entirely possible that the man who attends at every moment to the Lord may make business relationships mutually fruitful in the way that a good farmer makes his land and his neighbors' land fruitful. But he must ever set a watchman in his heart against the allure of riches and must ever remind himself of Adam Smith's opinion that it is not from the good will of the butcher or the baker that we get our meat and our bread, but from their hope of gain.[83] As long as our economy is founded chiefly on hope of gain rather than on desire to cultivate the goodness of the created world, the system of lending and investment will remain a key weapon in acedia's arsenal.

With Usura

If the economy of the modern world depends on mass migration to cities, on a departure from agricultural pursuits, and on an

---

[83] Adam Smith, *The Wealth of Nations* (London: Penguin, 1999), 119.

increased reliance on technology, it is the usurious stance—that is, the primacy of monetary gain as chief end of human life—which makes these things most critically dangerous by heightening their susceptibility to acedia. Many of the great cities of today, such as Rome, Paris, or London, had already established their greatness by the medieval age, calling people to themselves in large numbers. But their success, as Roger Scruton points out, was not dependent on economic excellence in the modern sense, but on their capacity to allow for human flourishing through a grand blending of domestic, artistic, commercial, and ecclesial concerns.[84] In fundamentally viable cities, we find cafes across the street from cathedrals, with park space in between, businesses scattered about, and homes tucked into the free corners. The modern habit of dividing our cities into business districts and suburbs and art quarters and so on has only served to accent the point that we come to the cities to make money, though we grudgingly cordon off those other spaces where man does the other things he must, including indulging in the impractical appreciation of art.

In an essay on the enduring importance of Dante and the *Divine Comedy*, Eugenio Montale suggests that it is just this difference—between cities directed to human flourishing and those directed to economic gain, between cultures founded on ideas and those founded on facts—that marks the great contrast between the medieval and the modern world.[85] The Edict of Milan, which granted tolerance to Christians in the Roman Empire, allowed the Church to emerge from the domus and fully engage civic

---

[84] Roger Scruton, *The Aesthetics of Architecture* (Princeton, NJ: Princeton University Press, 2013), xiii.

[85] Eugenio Montale, "Dante, Yesterday and Today," in *The Poets' Dante*, ed. Peter S. Hawkins and Rachel Jacoff (New York: Farrar, Straus, and Giroux, 2001), 113–114.

society such that cities like Florence and Paris could become great cultural centers despite the challenges of city life, which included plague, war, and greed. The Donation of Constantine, if itself a forgery, nonetheless drew out the lineaments of the religious-political reality, a reality of deep civic integration, which came to exist in the Middle Ages. On the other hand, the modern age has been one of disintegration. And whereas the *Divine Comedy* is a quintessentially medieval work—a poem of total integration, of the weaving of classical myth, scholastic theology, Italian politics, natural science, and practically everything else that could have been known to a Florentine of the early fourteenth century—the work of Shakespeare begins to demonstrate something of the modern disintegration that started with the Reformation and continues to our day, engendering those conditions in which "the center cannot hold," in which sloth flourishes and worship subsides.[86]

In *the Merchant of Venice*, we find one of literature's starkest representations of usury in the practices of Shylock the money-lender. The play's outset is colored by long-standing animosity between Shylock and a Venetian merchant, Antonio, the former a Jew and the latter a Christian. Partly as a function of his religion, Shylock is allowed to lend money at interest (Jews generally were, even in the midst of medieval Christian kingdoms that forbade the practice for Christians). Antonio, on the other hand, lends money gratis and brings down the rate of usury in Venice. When Antonio's friend Bassanio finds himself in need of ready funds to woo the fair lady Portia, and Antonio's money is currently all out in trade ventures, the pair turn to Shylock, who agrees to

---

[86] See Seamus Heaney, "Envies and Identifications," in *Poet's Dante*, 244.

loan Bassanio three thousand ducats, with Antonio as guarantor. The catch is that the interest is set at a pound of Antonio's flesh. When Antonio's ships founder at sea, Shylock delightedly calls in the bond and demands his pound, and it is only through Portia's legalistic intervention that Antonio is spared.

The case is curious for our purposes on two counts. First, it illustrates St. Jerome's contention that usury sucks at the life of the debtor. Here, of course, the case is quite literal. Antonio is all set to die when his investments fail, whereas the gnawing anxiety most modern Americans feel is the constant presence of debts extending into the vast sea of the future. How many lives are slowly worn away under the press of financial worry? Or how many have at last come to feel that their debts are too much to bear? A recent study shows that roughly 16 percent of suicides arise from financial anxiety.[87] When the mind is drawn on ceaselessly into a future which seems to hold no hope of salvation, the noonday devil has readied the ground for despair.

Secondly, Antonio's case serves as a reminder of the danger of an investment economy generally; at the very least, it urges us to remember that the only safe treasure is that stored up in Heaven. And the more we allow ourselves to be drawn out of the eternal present where such treasure is laid up, the more acedia makes us hate that very present. The eternal end of our life becomes repugnant when viewed against a temporal goal tied to earthly treasure. Perhaps this can supply one facet of the mood which overwhelms Antonio at the beginning of the play: "In sooth I know not why I

---

[87] Financial Security Program and Dyvonne Body, "The Burden of Debt on Mental and Physical Health," Aspen Institute, August 2, 2018, https://www.aspeninstitute.org/blog-posts/hidden-costs-of-consumer-debt/.

am so sad."[88] It is a mantra that sloth has made to fit the modern world.

A still more plain indictment of sloth comes three and a half centuries after Shakespeare, in the *Cantos* of Ezra Pound. Montale suggests that if the great text of the Middle Ages, in suggesting the integration of all aspects of life, was the *Divine Comedy*, Pound's epic is the great text of disintegration through its theme of usury, here laid out in biting detail:

With Usura

With usura hath no man a house of good stone
each block cut smooth and well fitting
that design might cover their face,
with usura
hath no man a painted paradise on his church wall
… where virgin receiveth message
and halo projects from incision,
with usura …
no picture is made to endure nor to live with
but it is made to sell and sell quickly
with usura, sin against nature,
is thy bread ever more of stale rags
is thy bread dry as paper,
with no mountain wheat, no strong flour
with usura the line grows thick
with usura is no clear demarcation
and no man can find site for his dwelling.
Stonecutter is kept from his stone
weaver is kept from his loom

---

[88] Shakespeare, *The Merchant of Venice*, 1.1.

WITH USURA
wool comes not to market
sheep bringeth no gain ... usura
blunteth the needle in the maid's hand
....
Usura rusteth the chisel
It rusteth the craft and the craftsman
It gnaweth the thread in the loom
None learneth to weave gold in her pattern;
Azure hath a canker by usura;
....
Usura slayeth the child in the womb
It stayeth the young man's courting
It hath brought palsey to bed, lyeth
between the young bride and her bridegroom
CONTRA NATURAM.[89]

Pound's knowledge of the tradition, like Dante's, is encyclopedic, and while we may easily get lost in his allusions, his point remains clear: usury, gnawing away at man's life by drawing him constantly into anxious care for the future and the past, attacks man teleologically, cutting him off from that full, contemplative flourishing which is meant for him on earth and in Heaven. It does so, in Pound's view, by three chief means: first, by eroding craftsmanship; second, by inhibiting man's capacity to dwell fruitfully in a place; and third, by interfering in the structures of family life.

By making monetary gain the highest good, usury rusts the chisel, gnaws the thread, blunts the needle, and kills the knowledge

---

[89] Ezra Pound, "With Usura," in *The Cantos of Ezra Pound* (New York: New Directions, 1996), 229-230.

of weaving tapestries with gold. Mass production of commodities from the cheapest possible materials by the cheapest possible labor leaves us with a world of furniture, clothing, books, appliances, and homes which wear out all too rapidly. A well-made dresser of oak or mahogany may last centuries; a dresser of particleboard may last a decade. And while fine craftsmen are still to be found, their numbers are few and their goods are of necessity priced beyond the reach of the average consumer.

Under such conditions, it is difficult for man to establish himself in a dwelling which allows him to flourish. With usury, we have no houses of good stone, with each face smoothed to receive that noble design which the great sixteenth-century art critic Giorgio Vasari described as the mark of Renaissance genius. Well-built houses permit the dweller a measure of freedom from worry about the structure itself. While all material is subject to decay, the man who lives in a finely constructed house of noble materials has less to fear from the elements than the man who lives in a mass-produced structure of cheap stuff. Then, too, usury often prevents those other elements of man's life which make his dwelling fruitful from possessing that beauty which should attend them. With usury, suggests Pound, the church walls lose their painted paradises. Our age has no shortage of the money needed to build beautiful churches and to decorate them according to the demands of the heavenly liturgy. But our ends are not those of the medieval man; our gaze is not set on eternal riches but on temporal ones, and we have cheapened our houses and God's in consequence.

~~Finally, usury creates conditions of temporal anxiety that cut at the roots of family life. How many women seek abortions due to financial fears? How many young men and women refuse to marry? How many husbands and wives lie awake at night, unable to enjoy~~

the marriage debt with one another for the weight of the financial debts pressing against them? How many families have been swept into the horizontal mindset that an investment economy husbands so that their driving concern is for future financial success rather than for constant attention to the Lord?

We are told that it is foolish even to suggest that the modern economy may stand counter to the Church's ancient prohibition against usury. We are reassured that Mother Church herself invests her money and that capitalistic development has voided the financial insecurity that so often made investments ruinous in the past. And indeed, the modern system works out to the advantage of many. Yet, around the reassurances that the modern way is the best way lingers a suggestion that "this is just the way we do things now, and if there are dangers in that way, it's too hard to change at this point."

Nonetheless, we ought at least to recognize that the modern economy, inasmuch as it looks to monetary gain as man's chief goal, will persist in being a key tool in acedia's belt, driving man to despise his eternal end and bidding him forget the Lord's Day in favor of another day's profit.

Sex and Existentialism

With the rise of the modern economy in its industrial and usurious aspects, we must still consider two other major shifts in modern life which have contributed to acedia's supremacy and the demise of the Lord's Day as a touchstone of cultural life. Both the philosophical transition to a thoroughly existentialist viewpoint and the sexual revolution have worked hand in hand with usury to turn modern man away from his proper end, which is best enjoyed on earth in the celebration of the liturgy as the supreme moment of Lord's Day rest.

The Philosophical Revolution

The modern, atheistic brand of existentialism may be summed up in a statement from Jean-Paul Sartre's 1946 lecture "Existentialism Is a Humanism." There, in a strong challenge to the classical understanding of man's telos, Sartre said, "There is no human nature because there is no God to think it creatively."[90] For the classical tradition, especially from Aristotle, we recall that a thing's nature is the inherent organizational principle which drives it to its end so that it operates in predictable ways. We have discussed this idea already: fire always rises, and a chair, which is made for someone to sit on, always performs that function, provided that it is well-made and that its materials are resilient. As you will recall, Aristotle says that man is directed toward happiness in contemplation. Sartre, looking back on a half-century of unimaginable violence, gives voice to what is perhaps a growing conviction amidst the general run of man: namely, that man has no such end. At the very least, he says, if man is on some level directed to happiness, that desire is oriented in an emptiness, such that, with God having been removed from the picture, it belongs to each man to forge whatever happiness he can by fashioning his own nature.

The effects of this stance are highly pronounced in our day, in everything from the modern obsession with self-discovery to the creation of personal brands on social media to the rise of transgender ideology and boutique in vitro fertilization practices. At every opportunity, we seek to fashion ourselves after our own image, according to our own likeness, frequently rebelling in the process

[90] Jean-Paul Sartre, "Existentialism Is a Humanism," quoted in Josef Pieper, *The Silence of St. Thomas: Three Essays*, trans. John Murray and Daniel O'Connor (South Bend, IN: St. Augustine's Press, 1999), 52–53.

against the natural order of creation. We recall that such rebellion, such hatred for the solid order of being, is a mark of acedia.[91]

It is not, of course, that such thinking is a modern invention. Existentialism in itself, though we tend to think it a kind of dirty word, has little moral inclination one way or another. We may fairly speak of a line of Christian existentialism running through certain books of Scripture, particularly Job and the Prophets, up through St. Augustine and on to Kierkegaard, Jacques Maritain, and the like. Nor is the virulent Sartrean existentialism of our day itself completely modern. We find an early iteration of it in the moral reasoning of Iago, the villain of Shakespeare's *Othello*. As Iago tells the lovesick Roderigo,

> Virtue? A fig! 'Tis in ourselves that we are thus or
> thus. Our bodies are our gardens, to the which our
> wills are gardeners. So that if we will plant nettles
> or sow lettuce, set hyssop and weed up thyme,
> supply it with one gender of herbs or distract it
> with many, either to have it sterile with idleness or
> manured with industry, why the power and corrigible
> authority of this lies in our wills.[92]

That is, our nature is what we would make of it, using our own will to fashion ourselves as we see fit. But Iago is the villain, whereas the Sartrean model has become the mainstay of much of modern discourse.

We can discern a critical thread in the development of the Sartrean model when we consider Giambattista Vico's Enlightenment dictum that it is only that which we make which we ever

---

[91] Snell, *Acedia and Its Discontents*, 59ff.
[92] Shakespeare, *Othello*, 1.3.

truly know.[93] This attitude, constitutive of the modern scientific theory, has, of course, critical applications for the experimental method, where we truly know the workings of the natural world by reproducing them. It is a fairly short step, however, from the use of experimental reproduction of phenomena to consolidate our knowledge of the physical world to the use of existential deployment of the will to fashion our own natures. Modern man is obsessed with the process of coming to know himself, of finding himself, of embarking on the journey of self-discovery. He rejects, though, the process of self-discovery through discovery of God and chooses instead to know himself by fashioning himself according to his own vision.

The Sexual Revolution

This atheistic existentialism is deeply intertwined with the sexual revolution. So-called sexual experiment and discovery have become crucial facets in the modern quest for personal identity, for fabrication of the self. ~~This is demonstrated in the transgender ideology which seeks to establish the individual as sole arbiter of his or her identity. We find in this a grand, satanic disdain for the order of being established by God's enduring creative action.~~ In it we find, too, a kind of false angelism. For it is the body, St. Thomas tells us, which serves as the individuating principle of man, whereas angels are distinguished according to their forms, their natures.[94] By seeking to be infinitely divisible according to form, mankind attempts to place itself on a level with the angels, further rejecting the hierarchy of being.

---

[93] See Brumfield, *Benedict Proposal*, 14–15.
[94] St. Thomas Aquinas, *Summa Theologica* I, q. 50, art. 2.

Likewise, as Pound indicates in his verses on usury, one of the major effects of the sexual revolution—and of acedia's grip on the modern world—has been the vast availability of abortion and contraception, both of which are used primarily to avoid the working of nature and to eschew temporal anxiety. Contraception and abortion, both tools for divorcing the conjugal act from its natural end, seek to give man the chance to "seize the moment," to enact a false escape from the anxiety we feel over the past and the future and to live fully in the now, giving ourselves over to the movements of the passions. Here again, we witness acedia's capacity for making the concrete reality of existence hateful. The child in the womb, which ought to be the cause of joy in the fulfillment of the offices of love, becomes instead an object of terror, an obstacle to happiness, a tumor which must be cut out. Complications of this sort having been avoided, the sexual act can become an easy means of fashioning our own nature through use of the other as a sexual object.

You Can't Repeat the Past: Jay Gatsby, the American Dream, and Acedia

To see how acedia, working within a modern economy and employing an atheistic drive to self-creation, has assumed command of the contemporary landscape, to the point of destroying the Lord's Day, we can do worse than to turn to the example of *The Great Gatsby*.

In what does Gatsby's greatness exist? It is primarily in what Nick Carraway, the novel's narrator, calls his infinite capacity for hope. And Gatsby hopes, above all, to win back the love of Daisy Fay, now Daisy Buchanan, whom Gatsby had known and loved as a poor, young army officer. During Gatsby's absence in the Great War, Daisy married Tom Buchanan of Chicago, and the two now enjoy one of the finest estates on Long Island, in patrician, old-money East Egg. Across Long Island Sound, in the nouveau riche, fantastical West Egg, Gatsby has purchased a Norman mansion where he hosts nightly parties of Trimalchian dimensions, entertaining senators and movie stars alongside bootleggers and the starry-eyed hangers-on of New York's glittering Jazz Age society. He maintains this fantastic menagerie in hope that Daisy will one night walk through his door and restore time to the joyous moment of five years prior, when the two gave themselves to each other in love and Gatsby wedded his Platonic dreams of glorious self-creation to Daisy's person.

The strength of acedia in America may be measured by three of Gatsby's qualities: first, by his love of money and his love of Daisy as the supreme representation of money; second, by his belief that money can allow man to escape the passage of time and the progression of nature; and third, by the absence of God from the moral and social landscape he inhabits.

The first thing we know about Gatsby is that he is immensely wealthy. His nightly expenditures rival those of the court of Solomon. His guests whisper that he has more money than God. He reminds Tom Buchanan that, as he's amassed as much wealth as Tom has, he's just as good as Tom is. And, most telling of all, he remarks to Nick on the last evening of his life that Daisy's voice is full of money. That, ultimately, is Daisy's value to Gatsby. She is an image of wealth, an image of the riches that would permit infinite self-definition. And this, after all, is the American dream: the idea that through hard work and a certain amount of luck and charm, we may become anything we wish to be. Thus, this dream, or at least a version of it, goes hand in hand with the kind of Sartrean existentialism which rebels against the concrete circumstances of life.

Part of Gatsby's love of money lies in his assumption, his deep hope, that through his money he will be able to repeat the past, to restore his life to that paradisal moment when he first knew Daisy and Daisy gave herself to him. Nick Carraway cautions Gatsby, "You can't repeat the past." Gatsby, incredulous, responds, "Why of course you can!"[95] Gatsby, like so many of his fellow Americans of our day, would have enough money to isolate himself from the anxiety of time—if such a thing were possible. Yet he finds that even his vast resources cannot do that. For the bond of human sexual love that he once had with Daisy and that he has again with her in adultery has also been shared between Daisy and Tom. In the latter case, though, this love has produced its natural end: a child. The cold, frozen moment of eternal human love which Gatsby wishes to seize in virtue of his riches forever eludes him. Human life is not, the child forces him to recognize, like the figures on a Grecian urn. Gatsby would have Keats's vision of the undying moment:

> Bold Lover, never, never canst thou kiss,
> Though winning near the goal yet, do not grieve;
> She cannot fade, though thou hast not thy bliss,
> For ever wilt thou love, and she be fair![96]

Yet time bears us on, ceaselessly into the past, as the novel tells us in its final line, as well as into the future. Our beauty fades, while in the sexual urge the next generation calls us to die. Acedia hates this death, hates the flow of time through which God's will calls us to union with him.

It is God who is most conspicuously absent from Gatsby's world. Other than the astonished whisper that Gatsby has more money

---

[95] F. Scott Fitzgerald, *The Great Gatsby* (New York: Scribner, 1995), 110.

[96] Keats, "Ode on a Grecian Urn," lines 17-20.

than God, the only mention of the Deity in the book comes from the half-crazed lips of George Wilson, who gazes out at a pair of massive eyes on a billboard, an advertisement for a now-defunct oculist, Dr. T. J. Eckleburg, and reminds us that God sees everything. The man beside George, glancing up at the sign, reminds him that that's just an advertisement.

This is the image of America and its dream, bequeathed to us by Fitzgerald. If New York, the pinnacle of America, is a successful city, as Scruton argues, then we find in Gatsby that its success, and, by extension, the success of the American Dream, is at best precarious. The golden land of J. P. Morgan and Midas is divided from the place where people spend themselves in the most stellar, blue, symphonic dissipation possible, and in between these two realms is a land of crumbling ash heaps where God looks on, reduced to a pair of spectacles on an abandoned billboard.[97] It is an image of a land overmastered by acedia, obsessed with defeating time by making a false eternity of the seized temporal moment, a land which sets its security in monetary wealth and in which worship has been forgotten.

The question, then, is how to shake off the noonday devil. If this devil makes us hate our proper good, then the cure must lie in turning joyfully to that proper good. The rest of this book seeks to clarify ways in which, restoring proper Lord's Day worship, modern man may cast off the pharaoh within. In order to do this, though, we must first seek to understand the Lord's Day itself, especially in relation to the Jewish Sabbath and the command to rest.

---

[97] Scruton, *Aesthetics of Architecture*, xiii.

3

Reclaiming Time: Sabbath and the Lord's Day

From our discussion of time thus far, it might be tempting to draw the conclusion that the solution to our modern maladies is to be found in seizing the moment. And we will see that there is a way of being attentive to the present moment, of carrying out the precise task demanded of us at all times, which is part of the way to holiness.[98] Yet such a way is far different from the contemporary craze for "living in the now," or by any other means eating, drinking, and making merry, by living in a brilliant sunshine of the present in order to forget that we will die.

Such a life is not scriptural in any holistic sense, nor is it Christian, inasmuch as we take the life of the Christian to be modeled on that of Christ. The Bible, though it constantly reads time in the light of eternity, is of all great works of literature perhaps the one most concerned with time. Genesis gives us time's beginning. Revelation shows us time's end. We are told the number of Adam's years and the years of Israel's enslavement in Egypt. The book of Kings supplies its rhythmic delineation of each king's reign. Scripture dwells

---

[98] Pierre de Caussade, *The Sacrament of the Present Moment*, trans. Kitty Muggeridge (San Francisco: Harper and Row, 1982), 1.

endlessly on the cycles of time, from the seven-day work of Creation to the three-day epiphanic sequences of Sinai, the wedding at Cana, and the Resurrection. The Gospels are filled with phrases such as "on the third day," "the next day," "it was then about noon," "from the sixth hour to the ninth hour," and "immediately."

Whereas the great Homeric epics exist in a kind of bright eternity always focused on the present temporal moment—the endless sunshine of figures on Grecian urns poised on the verge of battle or love—the Hebrew and Christian Scriptures hold up the present moment and its extensions against the dark, brooding background of eternity.[99] A figure like Odysseus is the true king of seizing the moment, of taking whatever time presents to him, whether it be a meal in the cave of a Cyclops or a year in the bed of Circe. The background of Penelope and Telemachus, of Laertes and Athena, fades away as he adventures across the Mediterranean. For a figure like Abraham, on the other hand, it is the eternal background of God that at every moment informs his temporal actions.

For the scriptural authors, then, life is not a matter of seizing the moment but of lifting every moment to eternity. The anxiety we experience as a result of time may, under this rubric, become a means of our being stretched with Christ on the Cross toward time's eternal limit. That is, the more biblical our outlook is, the more our consciousness will expand to the beginning and the end to embrace all in between as a gift of God—and as a sacrifice that the Son offers in His own body to the Father. Still, the temporal distension which all men experience as a prime cause of anxiety is not limited to those of us who sin. We see throughout the Gospels

---

[99] Erich Auerbach, "Odysseus' Scar," chap. 1 in *Mimesis: The Representation of Reality in Western Literature*, trans. Willard R. Trask (Princeton, NJ: Princeton University Press, 1968), 53–89.

that Jesus does not reduce His ministry to a kind of supreme living in the moment. On the contrary, He is deeply concerned with time, specifically with His hour. He reminds Mary of this during the wedding at Cana. He prophesies three times that He will suffer and die and on the third day be raised. In the Garden of Gethsemane, He looks ahead to His Passion in such agony that blood flows from His pores.

This is not to say that Jesus does not attend with the greatest intensity to the work of each moment. Though He is in some sense always attending to the hour of His being lifted up on the Cross, He attends as well to the sick and sinful herd which meets Him along the way. We witness a supreme example of Jesus' manner of attending to the present through the eternal in the story of the cure of Jairus's daughter and the woman with a hemorrhage (Luke 8:40-56). It's a masterpiece of storytelling. Jairus comes to Jesus, informs him that his daughter is sick, and asks Him to come and heal her. As the Lord passes through the crowd, a woman who has suffered for twelve years with a hemorrhage touches the hem of His garment and is cured, such that Jesus feels the power go out of Him and stops to ask who it was that touched Him.

It's a moment of the most excruciating temporal anxiety. We can feel the bewilderment of the apostles as they point out the great press of the crowd and ask how they could possibly know who touched Him. We can feel the distress of Jairus, waiting there as his daughter dies, time slipping inexorably away as Jesus stands there, letting the crisis drag on.

And then word comes: don't bother Jesus any longer. The girl has died. The time to save her has vanished into the past. Jesus reassures Jairus, and us, that the girl is not dead but sleeping. He proceeds to awaken her, and we breathe a sigh of relief with the astonished father.

It is not simply that Jesus knows that He can heal the girl. Rather, as He tells us, the God of Abraham, Isaac, and Jacob is not God of the dead but of the living (Mark 12:27). In eternity, the girl is always alive. Christ, in the midst of His humanity, looks nonetheless with the Father's eternal vision. It is this attention to the Father that allows Christ to keep His hour ever in mind even as He performs the work that every moment presents to Him. To be a Christian is in no small part to develop Christ's attention to eternity and so to equip ourselves for the work of the present. Above all, it is the Lord's Day which so equips us, teaching us to gather up all the time given us, and all the time given to creation, to lift all up to the Father, and so to participate in the eternal offering of love among the Persons of the Trinity.

The Roots of the Sabbath

All of time, from the beginning in Genesis to the end in Revelation, is a theater in which man offers worship. The vicissitudes of history may well be read as a chronicle of man's relative success and failure in offering right worship to God. Certainly the Old Testament supplies such a chronicle, with the great successes in Israel's history corresponding to those moments when the nation was most faithful to the Lord. It is not that God, feeling pettish about a scarcity of incense or bulls, spites His people in a fit of pique. Rather, failure to worship properly is failure to order the mind and heart to the order of reality. When our attention wanders from the supernatural, we fall out of step with the natural, and the natural consequences can be quite dire.

The great work of the Mosaic books, the dramatic action at the heart of the narrative, consists in the twofold labor of God's redeeming His people from the clutches of Pharaoh and the people learning how to worship God, with the result that the people become a new creation. With the redemption of the people comes also a suggestion of the redemption of creation itself; thus, St. Paul speaks of "hope that creation itself would be set free from slavery to corruption and share in the glorious freedom of the children of God" (Rom. 8:20-21). These three facets—the escape from Pharaoh, the proper worship, and the new creation—are intimately linked, as the Mosaic texts on the Sabbath indicate.

The first mention of what would become the Sabbath occurs in Genesis 2:2-3: "On the seventh day God completed the work he had been doing; he rested on the seventh day from all the work he had undertaken. God blessed the seventh day and made it holy, because on it he rested from all the work he had done in creation." God's rest is not a sudden cessation of His creative activity. As St. Thomas Aquinas notes, God is continuously maintaining creation. This rest is rather an ongoing contemplative joy in the fullness of creation.

Sabbath rest is next remembered in Exodus 16. Even prior to the delivery of the Ten Commandments at Sinai, the people are reminded of the need to imitate God in Sabbath rest in the regulations concerning manna.

> On the sixth day they gathered twice as much food, two omers for each person. When all the leaders of the community came and reported this to Moses, he told them, "That is what the LORD has prescribed. Tomorrow is a day of rest, a holy sabbath of the LORD. Whatever you want to bake, bake; whatever you want to boil, boil; but whatever is left put away and keep until the morning." When they put it away until the morning, as Moses commanded, it did not stink nor were there worms in it. Moses then said, "Eat it today, for today is the sabbath of the LORD. Today you will

not find any in the field. Six days you will gather it, but on the seventh day, the sabbath, it will not be there." Still, on the seventh day some of the people went out to gather it, but they did not find any. Then the LORD said to Moses: How long will you refuse to keep my commandments and my instructions? Take note! The LORD has given you the sabbath. That is why on the sixth day he gives you food for two days. Each of you stay where you are and let no one go out on the seventh day. After that the people rested on the seventh day. (16:22–30)

God has given the Israelites quail and manna in answer to their cries of complaint. Why, they ask, could they not have remained in Egypt with its slavery and its fleshpots? The hearts of the Israelites have grown accustomed to dependence on Pharaoh. Though their slavery was cruel, though their labors were doubled and redoubled, there remained nonetheless the abundance of Egypt.

The desert wandering trains Israel first in trusting the abundance of God, in recognizing that God has not only redeemed His people but has also ordered creation so that it will provide for them daily, superabundantly, extravagantly, with provision even for the people to abstain from labor on the seventh day. It takes time for the Israelites to understand this. Some of them try to save manna from one day to the next; others try to gather it on the seventh day. ~~Each such action betrays an inability to trust the Lord entirely.~~ Each marks a lingering prejudice in favor of the abundance of Pharaoh.

~~Such trust having been established, Israel can move toward authentic worship, with full recognition of the place of Sabbath rest.~~ The pattern of worship is established at Sinai, where the Israelites arrive after three months of wandering. In prototypical theophanic fashion, God descends upon the mountain on the third day and speaks to Moses the conditions of Israel's covenantal faithfulness: namely, the Ten Commandments. The third, the injunction to keep holy the Sabbath, is treated at second-greatest length of all the commandments:

> Remember the sabbath day—keep it holy. Six days you may labor and do all your work, but the seventh day is a sabbath of the LORD your God. You shall not do any work, either you, your son or your daughter, your male or female slave, your work animal, or the resident alien within your gates. For in six days the LORD made the heavens and the earth, the sea and all that is in them; but on the seventh day he rested. That is why the LORD has blessed the sabbath day and made it holy. (Exod. 20:8-11)

The third commandment brings together creation and Israel's redemption. No longer will the people work simply for the fulfillment of Pharaoh's desires, laboring to create garrisons and monuments for future wars and future remembrances of the kings of the past. Rather, they will dedicate themselves to God, resting every seventh day in imitation of the God who gazes upon the goodness of His creation. Every seventh day, the people will allow themselves to be made new through this contemplative imitation—which is also worship.

The pattern of creation and redemption continues when Moses goes up the mountain to receive the tablets on which God Himself has written the Commandments: "Moses went up the mountain. Then the cloud covered the mountain. The glory of the LORD settled upon Mount Sinai. The cloud covered it for six days, and on the seventh day he called to Moses from the midst of the cloud" (Exod. 24:15-16). Here the seventh day becomes the moment of communion between God and man. It is the moment when man, resting in the presence of the Lord, reorients himself properly to learn how to act and worship in accord with God's being. On the mountain, Moses receives not only the Ten Commandments, which detail the moral lineaments of Israel's life, but also the plan for the tabernacle, including the Ark, the table, the menorah, and the tent cloth. This tabernacle would become a sanctuary for the Lord, that He might dwell in the midst of the people (Exod. 25:8). The connection between the tabernacle as the dwelling of the Lord and the Sabbath as the center of worship is emphasized by the reiteration of the Sabbath command at the end of God's colloquy with Moses, immediately after the details for the construction of the tabernacle:

> The LORD said to Moses: You must also tell the Israelites: Keep my sabbaths, for that is to be the sign between you and me throughout the generations, to show that it is I, the LORD, who make you holy. Therefore, you must keep the sabbath for it is holiness for you. Whoever desecrates it shall be put to death. If anyone does work on that day, that person must be cut off from the people. Six days there are for doing work, but the seventh day is the sabbath of complete rest, holy to the LORD. Anyone who does work on the sabbath day shall be put to death. So shall the Israelites observe the sabbath, keeping it throughout their generations as an everlasting covenant. Between me and the Israelites it is to be an everlasting sign; for in six days the LORD made the heavens and the earth, but on the seventh day he rested at his ease. (Exod. 31:12-17)

The Sabbath injunction thus frames the covenant at Sinai. It marks the beginning of Israel's dependence on God in the collection of the manna. It rests at the heart of the Ten Commandments.

And it orders all of the moral and liturgical activity enjoined on Israel through Moses on the mountain. The creative pattern that God established in the beginning is to be the embodied cultural sign whereby Israel will show itself to be set apart by God, made holy by Him and utterly dependent on Him for its existence. Thus, Israel shall be for all the world a beacon of God's creative activity, activity which never ceases and which is fulfilled in the redemptive labors of the Word.

Christ and the Sabbath

In the New Covenant, Christians no longer observe the seventh-day Sabbath of the Jews. Rather, in honor of Christ's Resurrection, we celebrate the Lord's Day on the first day of the week. Nonetheless, Christian observance of the Lord's Day subsumes and elevates the Jewish Sabbath and in so doing fulfills the commandment to keep holy the Sabbath day, which is not abnegated by the New Covenant. And, if we are to honor the Sabbath, we would do well to attend closely to Jesus' Sabbath practices.

Among all His actions, these are some of the most bitterly contested by the scribes and Pharisees. He persists in healing on the Sabbath, in letting his disciples pick heads of grain, perhaps at times in traveling beyond the traditional Sabbath day's journey allowed by the law. Especially in an age like ours, when the thought of abstaining from anything at all on the Sabbath feels so alien, the Pharisees' objections to Jesus' Sabbath works can seem bewildering, if not laughable, a feeling which can easily extend to the practices still current among some Orthodox Jews.

Perhaps our reaction might abate in some measure when we remember the importance of the Sabbath ordinances delivered in Exodus. The Sabbath was to be the principal sign by which Israel showed itself marked by God, subject to Him rather than to a king.

Adherence to the law was the means by which Israel could remain under God's wing. If picking heads of grain on the Sabbath seems a minuscule matter to us, we might recall that Israel was not allowed to collect manna on the Sabbath. If adherence to the law seems to us an irrelevant obsession, we might remember that failure to observe the law had led again and again to Israel's defeat in battle, to destruction of the Temple, to new imprisonment. And the shadow of the new pharaoh in Rome loomed large over Israel in Jesus' day.

Nonetheless, Christ leads Israel to a renewed understanding of Sabbath holiness as a participation in the ongoing creative fullness of God's contemplative life. One Gospel text in particular may serve as programmatic for Jesus' Sabbath labor and our imitation thereof. John 5 begins with the deeply moving narrative of Christ's healing the paralytic at the pool of Bethesda. The man had suffered thirty-eight years with his affliction, and there was no one to move him into the pool when it was agitated by the presence of the Spirit. In this pool, we might find an image of the void over which the Spirit broods in Genesis 1, with the crowds of sick at its side like so many signs of fallen creation, groaning toward renewal after the fashion St. Paul describes in his Letter to the Romans. Christ heals the paralytic and sends him on his way. The healed man is accosted by the Pharisees, who remind him that it is unlawful to carry his mat on the Sabbath. He can only respond, ignorant of Christ's identity, that the man who healed him told him to take up his mat and walk. Once the Pharisees learn that it was Jesus who healed him, they confront him: "Therefore, the Jews began to persecute Jesus because he did this on a sabbath. But Jesus answered them, 'My Father is at work until now, so I am at work.' For this reason the Jews tried all the more to kill him, because he not only broke the sabbath but he also called God his own father, making himself equal to God" (John 5:16–18).

It is Jesus' response, "My Father is at work until now, so I am at work," that so profoundly reveals the difference between the stultified vision of Sabbath rest which had arisen in Israel and the fullness of that rest as participation in the divine life to which God has called us from the beginning. The work of Creation, as noted above, does not simply stop on the seventh day. For one thing, as Snell notes, the text of Genesis indicates that "On the seventh day God completed the work he had been doing."[100] The seventh day marks the moment when God brings His work to completion and then rests in contemplation of Himself. Because God is the cause of His work, in contemplating Himself He is also contemplating the work, whose being He constantly maintains. The rest of the seventh day is thus the rest of the enduring ordinance of reality.

Christ's Sabbath labors, then, constitute an ongoing participation in that work of ordering reality. Where there is formlessness, as in an eye stricken with blindness, He, the eternal Word, through which the Father spoke creation into being, brings form. Where there is imperfection, as with a paralytic, He brings perfection. Where there is the lack of being which we call evil, He brings goodness, renewing the things of the world in accord with the goodness that the Father eternally observes and brings about.

The idea that Christ's ministry, including His Sabbath healings, should continue the labor of the Father, who of course does not exist in time but in the eternal now of which Sabbath rest is a foretaste, is reinforced by the way John introduces Christ's public ministry at the wedding at Cana. We are told that this wedding is held on the third day, the day of epiphany, the day on which God descended upon Sinai and the day on which Christ would rise from the dead. Moreover, the wedding may be taken as symbolic of the sixth day

---

[100] See Gen. 2:2; Snell, *Acedia and Its Discontents*, 106.

of the Creation account, when man and woman were made. By beginning His public ministry at a wedding, at the pinnacle, as it were, of creation, Christ signals that He is continuing the creative labor of His Father. This work has not yet been perfected at the time of Cana, though. The six stone water jars whose contents Christ would turn to the richest wine signify that the abundance of life (the fullness represented by the number seven) has not yet been bestowed on man. That would come at the wedding which concludes Christ's Passion, His marriage to the Church.

The Sabbath is mentioned infrequently, though with immense significance, throughout the rest of John's Gospel. In John 7:21-22, Christ, interrogated by the Jewish leaders, refers to His healing of the paralytic as the reason for their discontent with Him. Master of the law that Christ is, though, He in turn questions the Pharisees on their own Sabbath practices, reminding them that they themselves will circumcise a child on the Sabbath should the appointed day coincide with the Sabbath feast. In John 9, Christ heals another man on the Sabbath, making a paste of saliva and clay to smear on the man's eye and restore his sight. Again, the narrative is pregnant with memories of Genesis, with the creation of man out of clay and the emergence of new life from the watery chaos of the pool of Siloam. In John 12:1, Christ comes to Bethany for His last visit with His friends prior to His Passion. We are told that this takes place six days before Passover, and, if Passover fell on a Friday, that would place the visit to Bethany, as Scott Hahn notes, on the Sabbath.[101] If so, this would make that least meal at Bethany particularly important for interpreting a Christian way of

---

[101] *The Ignatius Catholic Study Bible: The New Testament*, with introduction, commentary, and notes by Scott Hahn and Curtis Mitch (San Francisco: Ignatius Press, 2010).

honoring the Sabbath, as it is the last Sabbath to take place before the transformation of the Sabbath through Christ's death and Resurrection. We will return to this passage in a later chapter, when we consider the importance of family and friends in celebration of the Lord's Day. Finally, there is the dreadful Sabbath of Christ's entombment and descent into the realm of the dead, followed by the transformation of the first day of the week through His Resurrection. On that day, Christ appears first to Mary Magdalene and then to the apostles. A week later, He appears once again, this time when Thomas is present.

We will treat the Lord's Day shortly, but for now let it suffice to say that Christ's labor, which encompasses the Sabbath as a demonstration of God's ongoing work of causing the universe to be, gives way to the timelessness of the resurrected Lord, who invites us, as it were, into the eighth day—that reality in which space and time are drawn up eternally and glorified into the presence of the Lord.

The other Gospels give plentiful examples of the kind of work Christ does on the Sabbath, that work of restoring nature to its original order and preparing it for glorification in the resurrection.

Mark's Gospel almost immediately shows Jesus in the midst of Sabbath labor. After Christ has been baptized, gone into the wilderness, and called the first apostles, He comes to Capernaum, where He enters the synagogue on the Sabbath and teaches. The rest of the chapter unfolds so quickly that it is easy to lose sight of the fact that Jesus does an enormous amount of work on this single Sabbath. He cures a man with an unclean spirit. He then heals Simon's mother-in-law (who, we should recognize, immediately gets up and waits upon the Master, providing a rich model in her own right for Sabbath labor). Evening comes and He heals all the sick and possessed brought to Him from the whole town, which has gathered at the door. Mark 1 thus supplies us with a beautiful portrait of the transition from Old Testament Sabbath worship to the kind of Sabbath worship enjoined on Christians. Whereas Christ goes into the synagogue with the rest of Israel, His labor of restoring Israel to freedom and health then calls all the people to come to Him. He becomes the new temple, in whose person worship and thus all of creation is summoned to a higher pitch of being.

In Mark 2, we witness the disciples picking heads of grain on the Sabbath, and we hear Jesus' reply to the Pharisees, reminding them that David himself consumed the showbread in his hour of need. It is here that He declares that "the sabbath was made for man, not man for the sabbath. That is why the Son of Man is lord even of the sabbath" (27–28). And in Mark 3:5, having once again entered the synagogue on the Sabbath, Christ heals a man with a withered hand, saying "Stretch out your hand." There is an echo here of God's words to Moses, suggesting that in healing and restoring order on the Sabbath, Christ is likewise making us fit to carry out the prophetic and priestly work to which God has called us as fellow laborers in the vineyard. Finally, we find in Mark 6 the account of Jesus' rejection at Nazareth, when He enters the synagogue and reads from Isaiah, only to be rejected by the people, unable to work many miracles on account of their lack of faith.

Matthew likewise shares the story of the disciples picking the heads of grain on the Sabbath. Other than that, the Sabbath is directly mentioned but little, except for in Christ's description of the end times, when He bids His followers pray that it will not occur on the Sabbath, presumably so that there would not be strife between those who wish to flee and those who refuse on the grounds of the Sabbath commandment. Nonetheless, Matthew exhibits a supreme concern with the kind of spiritual outlook which should characterize the Christian. This is nowhere more evident than in the Beatitudes, specifically in the first: Blessed are the poor in spirit, for theirs is the Kingdom of Heaven. While every other beatitude looks forward to a future blessing—they will be comforted, they will be satisfied, they will inherit the land—this first one indicates a present blessing. The one who is poor in spirit is not simply humble, nor does he merely live a kind of internal poverty; rather, he recognizes that everything he has and is comes from God, that he is dependent on God for every moment of his existence. By doing so, he makes himself present to the God who sustains him and begins to enjoy the blessing of heavenly existence insofar as this life allows.[102] And it is exactly this kind of presence that Jesus exemplifies, doing the work of the Father and then retiring to prayerful communion with Him. That is the Sabbath rest to which we are called.

Luke first mentions the Sabbath in the account of Jesus' rejection at Nazareth, which is followed by a portrayal of Jesus' Sabbath work of teaching, healing, and driving out demons (4:16-41). Luke 6:1-11 presents various debates about the Sabbath, prompted by the picking of the heads of grain. In Luke 13:10-17, Jesus heals a woman crippled by a spirit for eighteen years, unable to stand erect. In this, the Sabbath once again becomes a moment of demonstration of the creative power of God, restoring mankind to the stature meant for him in Eden. Finally, in Luke 14:1-6, Christ heals the man with dropsy.

Throughout the Gospels, then, we find Christ extending an invitation to enter the Sabbath more deeply, not merely to engage

---

[102] See Sr. Anna Marie McGuan's illuminating podcast, *Scripture and the Spiritual Life*, particularly the episodes on Matthew 5.

with creation by resting in the creative love of the Father but to join with the Father in contemplating the goodness of the world and in continuing to order the world, restoring it to its original excellence and elevating it for its final life as part of the Kingdom. Ultimately, this kind of Sabbath observance, the rest of the seventh day, gives way in Christ's Resurrection to the glorious life of the Lord's Day.

The End of the Gospels: From Sabbath to the Lord's Day

While Christians continue to honor the Sabbath by keeping the Lord's Day, and while many Jews observe the Sabbath in keeping with the custom of some three thousand years, we may nonetheless legitimately speak of the last of all Sabbaths, the one on which Christ Himself takes the rest of death, the one on which His followers await the coming of the first day that they might rush to His tomb at dawn. We are speaking, of course, of that Sabbath from the dark of Good Friday to the dawn of Easter Sunday, when Christ lay in the shared tomb of Joseph of Arimathea and harrowed Hell, going to the limit of the kenotic descent from the Father's side.

Scripture itself tells us little of this Sabbath. We know that the disciples rested on that day in honor of the commandment. We know that the tomb was guarded at the request of those who feared the disciples would steal the body of Christ. Otherwise, the Gospel writers are silent on the matter.

Other ancient sources draw us imaginatively into Christ's descent among the dead, most prominently that ancient homily included in the Office of Readings for Holy Saturday. "What is happening?" the text asks. "Today there is a great silence over the earth, a great silence, and stillness, a great silence because the King sleeps; the earth was in terror and was still, because God slept in the flesh and raised up those who were sleeping from the ages.

God has died in the flesh, and the underworld has trembled."[103] The ensuing encounter between Christ and Adam, when Adam at last learns the extent of that contemplative rest to which God called him in the beginning, is among the most touching in world literature.

> I command you: Awake, sleeper, I have not made you to be held a prisoner in the underworld. Arise from the dead; I am the life of the dead. Arise, O man, work of my hands, arise, you who were fashioned in my image. Rise, let us go hence; for you in me and I in you, together we are one undivided person.
>
> For you, I your God became your son; for you, I the Master took on your form; that of slave; for you, I who am above the heavens came on earth and under the earth; for you, man, I became as a man without help, free among the dead; for you, who left a garden, I was handed over to Jews from a garden and crucified in a garden.
>
> Look at the spittle on my face, which I received because of you, in order to restore you to that first divine inbreathing at creation. See the blows on my cheeks, which I accepted in order to refashion your distorted form to my own image.[104]

This last Sabbath, this memorial of the day on which God completed His labors and rested from them, is the one on which the Word descends into the underworld and completes that labor once

---

[103] "The Lord's Descent into Hell," A Reading from an Ancient Homily for Holy Saturday, https://www.vatican.va/spirit/documents/spirit_20010414_omelia-sabato-santo_en.html.
[104] Ibid.

and for all, not simply restoring Adam to life in the garden but exalting him to life in Paradise. The ultimate Sabbath rest is the ultimate work of restoration, perfectly unifying the Maker and His image so that the cherubim who once guarded the gate of Eden will now indeed fall down before man as before the throne of God.

On the next day, the first day of the week—the Lord's Day—the biblical account resumes. Matthew presents the day succinctly in the final chapter of his Gospel. Mary and Mary Magdalene, coming to the tomb early in the morning, are greeted with an earthquake as an angel descends, rolls back the stone, and sits upon it, causing the guards to become like dead men. (Their reaction, reflective of both typical human astonishment at such a scene as well as, perhaps, their apprehension in guarding against the promised miracle, speaks to the hard-heartedness of our own time, in which we so often guard our hearts against the Resurrection by refusing to celebrate the Lord's Day.) The angel urges the women to go and tell the disciples to meet Jesus in Galilee, where the Lord greets them on the mountain and commissions them to go forth and make disciples of all nations.

The Marcan conclusion is somewhat more diffuse, with a shorter ending describing only the angel's appearance to the women at the tomb and a longer ending briefly describing Christ's appearance to Mary Magdalene and again to two disciples outside of town, and later to the Eleven, before commissioning them and ascending into Heaven.

Luke supplies the most detailed account yet, beginning with a similar description of the women's arrival at the tomb, where two men in dazzling garments appear and assure them that the Lord is risen. Returning to Jerusalem and repeating this message, they are met with the apostles' disbelief. Later, on the road to Emmaus, two disciples meet the Lord, who unfolds the meaning of

Scripture for them in a manner consonant with Jesus' authoritative preaching. It is not until the Lord breaks bread with them, though, that they recognize Him. Christ then appears to the rest of the disciples in the Upper Room in Jerusalem, eating a piece of baked fish and opening their minds to understand the Scriptures. Then He promises them the Holy Spirit, walks out with them to Bethany, and ascends.

John offers the lengthiest description of the Lord's Resurrection and its aftermath. He begins in much the same manner, with Mary Magdalene approaching the tomb and finding it empty. He then includes an account of John and Peter rushing to the tomb and facing the same discovery. As they return to Jerusalem, Mary waits, weeping, at the tomb. Looking into the empty space, she is surprised to see two angels sitting on the place where Jesus had lain, one at the head and one at the feet. John's description here immediately calls to mind the Ark of the Covenant, with its golden cherubim at either end. Jesus Himself appears to Mary, though she mistakes Him for the gardener; for us, this aligns Christ yet again with Adam—the man given to till and keep Eden. Jesus then appears to the disciples, next to Thomas, and finally to seven disciples at the Sea of Tiberias, where Peter atones for his threefold denial.

These stories are familiar enough. We set them here alongside one another for the sake of highlighting certain key patterns which can reflect contemporary challenges to worship. The first point, shared across all four accounts, is the critical fact that Christ is never seen in the tomb. *Resurrexit, sicut dixit*; He has risen, as He said. The angels present at the tomb have the joyous responsibility of heralding the Lord's Resurrection as well as reminding all who come, with perhaps a hint of jovial rebuke, that Christ Himself had promised this Resurrection, this rebuilding of the temple in three days. What is more, however early Mary Magdalene arrives at the tomb—and she seems to have arrived at the earliest possible moment allowed by Sabbath law—the Lord has risen first. We are always, in the doubt that draws us back to the place of death and in the duty that leads us promptly to the Lord, preceded by Christ.

Another prominent feature of each account is the doubt the disciples find so hard to overcome. Though they had followed Christ for three years, though they had watched Him raise Lazarus, restore sight to the blind, and feed multitudes, the disciples struggle in varying degrees to believe that the Lord has risen or, in some cases, to recognize Him. We can understand this doubt. Our tentative hearts grope with great difficulty toward belief in the most wondrous things. Our awareness of the world's hardness and of our own spiritual meagerness so often slithers through our minds with echoes of the serpent's words in Eden: Did Christ really mean He would rise again? Was His flesh really true food for the life of the world? Could you possibly be party to the wonder and joy of His Resurrection?

Finally, each Resurrection narrative contains a call to spread the astonishment of this most fundamental of human events. The rapid expansion of the Church in the apostolic era testifies to the sublime power of the Lord's Day to transform the doubting heart, conforming it to Christ's in a way that demands that same kind of wondrous labor that defined Christ's ministry. Those who serve as witnesses to the Resurrection, having been sealed with the Holy Spirit, go from being the fearful, frequently stumbling followers of Christ to acting very much like the Lord Himself: curing the sick, giving sight to the blind, being bitten by serpents but suffering no harm, and even raising the dead.

~~Our careless age knows little of this kind of witness.~~ Yet such testimony to the life-giving power of God is the birthright of all those who are baptized into Christ. ~~If the kind of spiritual energy~~

which pervades the Acts of the Apostles, the letters of Paul, and the book of Revelation eludes us today, it is perhaps precisely because we have abandoned the kind of spiritual mechanics that informed the day-to-day lives of Christians in that age. As we prepare to examine means to the restoration of the Lord's Day as a key to throwing off sloth, we turn to the last books of the New Testament for insight into the way observance of both the Jewish Sabbath and the Lord's Day served as a spiritual anchor for the early Church.

Acts of the Apostles: Living the Lord's Day throughout the Week

To answer the Lord's call, "Come, follow me," is by no means to commit to a single hour of worship per week. For the apostles, it meant leaving behind occupations, families, and houses, not to mention, in many cases, a good standing in the community, riches, and comfort. It meant leaving Capernaum and Jerusalem for Rome, Greece, Turkey, and India. It meant, in almost every case, martyrdom. It meant that every hour of every day, every encounter and every pursuit, could no longer be a matter of personal inter-est; rather, it had to become a moment of attention to the Lord as a fellow laborer in the Father's vineyard, seeking to bring about the Kingdom. Bringing about the Kingdom cannot be a matter of compartmentalization, of occasional prayer, occasional worship, occasional service, all quite comfortably separated from the real business of life. For Sts. Peter and Paul, life became a matter of prayer without ceasing, of dedication of every action and thought, of every moment of being, to the Father with the Son who had Himself lifted up all the world on the altar of the Cross.

How did the apostles sustain this life of total dedication to Christ? In the first place, their energy was no doubt a function of the depth of their encounters with the Lord, whose life became in them a spring welling up to eternal life, so that, through the exigencies of life, St. Paul could write, "I have learned, in whatever situation I find myself, to be self-sufficient. I know indeed how to live in humble circumstances; I know also how to live with abundance. In every circumstance and in all things I have learned the secret of being well fed and of going hungry, of living in abundance and of being in need. I have the strength for everything through him who empowers me" (Phil. 4:11–13).

This self-sufficiency was, in itself, a matter of recognizing Christ in the depth of selfhood, and this was a matter of prayer. One of the things that grows most striking about the account of St. Paul's travels in Acts is the manner in which he apparently maintains both the Sabbath and the Lord's Day as a joint locus of prayerful community which could expand the Body of Christ through Scripture and reason, strengthening that Body through partaking of the Eucharist. Again and again throughout his journeys, we are told that Paul goes to the synagogue on the Sabbath. There he enters into discussions on the Scriptures and seeks to persuade all present of the necessity of Christ's Incarnation, death, and Resurrection. And, at least in Acts 20, Paul breaks bread with the local church on the first day of the week, preaching so far into the night that the young man Eutychus, dozing off at the window, falls to his death, only to be restored when Paul throws himself down upon him. The eucharistic celebration then continues until dawn. "And they took the boy away alive and were immeasurably comforted" (12). Would that all Christians in their celebration of the Lord's Day could go away more alive, comforted beyond measure.

This Sabbath study of Scripture, followed by the Lord's Day Eucharist, must have served as a font of spiritual energy to St. Paul as, throughout the week, he debated, labored, wrote, and, in so many cases, endured persecution. Immersed in the Lord, attentive always to the working of the Spirit, Paul was at last strengthened for the martyrdom of decapitation which awaited him in Rome. The executioner's sword fell, and it is said that in the three places where his fallen head struck the ground, springs of water arose. He himself had caused a literal font of living water, welling up to eternal life. His death, whereby he entered that Lord's Day in which he had striven to live, continues to strengthen Christ's Church.

Revelation: The Heavenly Liturgy

The only apostle not to suffer martyrdom (though not for lack of attempts) was St. John, who ended his life in exile on the island of Patmos. There, the beloved disciple, the one who stood by Mary's side at the Crucifixion, the one who raced ahead of St. Peter to the tomb, the one who first recognized the Lord on the shore of the Sea of Tiberias, was "caught up in spirit on the Lord's day (Rev. 1:10). The ensuing encounter with one who looked like "a Son of Man" (Rev. 1:13) recalls the encounters with Christ on the day of the Resurrection. St. John falls like a dead man, just as the guards who were watching over the tomb fell at the sight of the angels.[105] The glory of the Lord, who appears as He did at the Transfiguration, His clothes dazzling white and His face shining like the sun at its brightest, overwhelms even the apostle who lay his head on Jesus' breast at the Last Supper.

After the Lord delivers messages to John for the angels of the seven churches of Asia, He calls John up to a vision of the throne of God and the heavenly worship that eternally attends it. Twenty-four

---

[105] We also recall the many times when Dante falls "as a corpse falls" in the *Inferno*. While these fits may be attributed to Dante's moral infirmity at that stage in his epic, it could also be argued that even in the *Inferno*, what he encounters is the Love of God, here alive in the infernal justice which attends the damned.

elders, as well as four animals, six-winged and covered in eyes, sing praise to the Lord; the animals proclaim without ceasing "Holy, holy, holy is the Lord God almighty, who was, and who is, and who is to come" (Rev. 4:8). Meanwhile the elders announce, "Worthy are you, Lord our God, to receive glory and honor and power, for you created all things; because of your will they came to be and were created" (Rev. 4:11). The heavenly praises emphasize the eternity of God as well as the created universe's utter dependence on Him, a dependence that is oriented toward worship as the true joy of all created beings. Indeed, at the approach of the Lamb, John "heard every creature in heaven and on earth and under the earth and in the sea, everything in the universe, cry out: 'To the one who sits on the throne and to the Lamb be blessing and honor, glory and might, forever and ever'" (Rev. 5:13).

While we tend to think of Revelation as an account of a future event, a final horrific drawing back of the curtain between time and eternity, John's vision of the heavenly liturgy serves as a reminder that eternity is not merely what awaits us at the end of time. Rather, eternity is the unbounded now of the Trinity, the perfect presence of Father, Son, and Holy Spirit, one to the other, which sustains creation and elicits the praises of the angelic choirs. The Lord's Day is God's weekly invitation to join that eternal chorus. It is the eternal, proffered to us in our temporal state. It is, as it were, the eighth day, the day on which the Lamb who was slain is raised to eternal life so that we, partakers of His flesh and blood, may likewise share in that life.

Man is made for the eternity of the Lamb, and all of man's life ought to be a process of submitting to that grace that makes eternity a possibility for our limited temporal selves. The Lord's Day, when the Passion and Resurrection are made present for us again and again until the end of time, is the supreme means by which God makes us one with Him, calling us back to the paradisal stewardship offered to Adam, consecrating creation as a cosmic temple, and raising man even beyond the scope of the angels. Yet modern man has lost his ear for the eternal music, has lost his taste for that flesh which is true food and that blood which is true drink. He has fallen under the spell of acedia, which rejects the command to rest in the presence of the Lord, which makes man hate that which is his proper end.

The way forward, then, is to return to God's presence by a renewed celebration of the Lord's Day. The rest of this book seeks to supply means for that return. It seeks, in the first place, to restore a vision of the liturgy as participation in the heavenly liturgy which at all times gives forth joyous shouts that echo in the roots of all the universe.

4

Saecula Saeculorum: Liturgy as Telos

He fathers forth whose beauty is past change: praise Him.
—Gerard Manley Hopkins, "Pied Beauty"

So far, we have said a great deal about anxiety and time, yet we have little mentioned time's concomitant: change. Experience of change, like time, runs the gamut of human faculties. On one hand, the anxiety man feels as a result of being drawn apart in time, torn between the past and the future, is in its way a function of a fundamental unease over change. Creatures of habit, many of us gravitate toward the status quo, with a sense that change is for the worse. Some people enjoy wondrous changes from bad luck to good, but, individually, we imagine that we could hardly hope to be fortune's beneficiaries.

Simultaneously, however, there is part of us that delights in change, in the kaleidoscopic flux of this realm of becoming which ensures that even our dullest moments are colored by the possibility that something might change, that there is something just beyond tomorrow which will sweep us along into the sublime reaches of human experience. And many spiritual writers have seen in time and its attendant changes the very means of God's working within us. "To live is to change," wrote John Henry Newman, "and to be perfect is to have changed often."[106]

The latter notion at once accords with and sharply diverges from a modern sensibility. On one hand, acedia itself prompts a sickly love of change, a sense that if we could only find a more suitable job, a more stimulating community, a holier parish, a better monastery, and so on, we could become who we are meant to be. Modern man, detesting boredom, is constantly bored, and seeks myriad means of shaking off his ennui.[107] On the other hand, the perfection that Newman descries at the end of life's change is itself anathema. "Nobody's perfect," the last hilarious utterance of *Some Like It Hot*, has become the motto of modern man, a verbal balm for all possible mediocrities. The perfection which Christ enjoins upon us and which Newman urges us toward seems to many today to demand the death of freedom, the forfeiture of all personality, the abandonment of all that frenetic change which makes life bearable.

Yet the final beatitude, which is man's call, consists in dwelling changelessly with that Father whose beauty is past change. Aristotle saw that the highest human activity was that timeless contemplation which is the nearest man may come to the eternal life of God. And the Church, aided by the light of faith, goes beyond Aristotle's vision to one of personal immortality which shares in the Resurrection of Christ in order to partake of the eternal feast

---

[106] Quoted in Stephanie Mann, " 'To Live Is to Change': My New View of Bl. John Henry Newman," October 9, 2016, *National Catholic Register*, https://www.ncregister.com/blog/to-live-is-to-change-my -new-view-of-bl-john-henry-newman.

[107] For wondrously humorous reading, consult *Ennui to Go: The Art of Boredom*, by Jon Winokur (Seattle: Sasquatch Books, 2005).

of trinitarian love. This is perfection. This is what it means to be made whole through God's covenantal action.

~~But we who occupy the earthly vale tend to know little of contemplation or eternity. For many of us, the kind of changelessness we associate with Heaven conjures up visions of the most deplorable boredom.~~ How can an eternity of worship fulfill my deepest longings and assuage my deepest hurts? How can anything be so delightful or engrossing as to bear eternal enjoyment? How could Heaven be something like a never-ending Mass?

This is in many ways the crux of the matter. The apocalyptic vision of St. John reveals to us the eternal liturgy of the Lamb who was slain on the altar of the Cross. What revelation reveals is the heavenly Mass, initiated on earth in Christ's Passion, death, and Resurrection, and made present until the end of the ages on the altars of Catholic churches the world over. The wonders presented to St. John comprise the reality unfolding before us at each liturgical celebration. But we do not have eyes to see. We doze off as the homily drags on, we desperately check our watches, and we rush off in relief when the final blessing is said, if we have lasted that long, or if we have come to Mass at all. What accounts for this disjunct between the reality of Mass and our experience thereof?

With these pervading questions of time, change, and liturgy, we are confronted with a constitutive element of authentic life in Christ: festivity. Indeed, the rest of this book may be taken as an attempt to restore festivity in modern life through proper celebration of the Lord's Day. Festivals mark those times set apart, those sacrificial moments of the year, when we look beyond the seemingly interminable business of life in this realm of becoming and toward the eternal joy of what truly is. The principal festival of the Church is Easter, and with it every Lord's Day, and in turn all celebrations of the Mass. A proper understanding of the Mass as the moment of sacrificial rest in which we offer ourselves on the altar with God and in turn are made one with Him, will allow us to overcome the fundamental tension between our experience of time and our expectation of eternity.

We will explore the question in three phases. First, we will consider in brief the role of the Mass in forming the Body of Christ. Second, we will examine what it is about human nature generally, and about modern life in particular, which makes the Mass, and the things of eternity, difficult for man to attend to. This part of our inquiry will echo much of what has been said about modern man's struggle with acedia, for man's tendency to sloth and his struggle to attend to the liturgy hinge on the same fault lines in his spiritual makeup. Third, we will examine the influence of the Second Vatican Council, considering the ways in which it attempted to address the very problem we are concerned with, the respects in which its reforms were co-opted into failure, and the capacities in which its documents nonetheless provide clues to restoring liturgical participation to a vital state.

The Body of Christ

The Council of Trent gives eloquent expression to the dynamism at the heart of the Mass:

> He, therefore, our God and Lord, although He was about to offer Himself once on the altar of the cross unto God the Father, by means of His death, there to operate *an eternal redemption*; nevertheless, because that His priesthood was not to be extinguished by His death, in the last supper, on the night in which He was betrayed, to the end that He might leave to His own beloved spouse the Church, a visible

sacrifice, such as the nature of men requires, whereby that bloody [sacrifice], once to be accomplished on the cross, might be represented, and the memory thereof remain even unto the end of the world, and its salutary virtue be applied unto the remission of those sins which we daily commit, declaring Himself constituted *a priest for ever, after the order of Melchisedech*, He offered up to God the Father His own body and blood under the species of bread and wine; and, under the symbols of those same things, He delivered [them] to be received by His apostles, whom He then constituted priests of the New Testament; and by those words, *This do in remembrance of me*, He commanded both them and their successors in the priesthood, to offer [them], as the Catholic Church has always understood and taught.[108]

In offering His own body upon the altar of the Cross, Christ at last renders up that perfect sacrifice wherein the demands of justice and mercy are met: justice inasmuch as through the hypostatic union mankind, in the Person of the Son of Man, is at last able to bear the full weight of punishment; mercy inasmuch as that same hypostatic union, uniting man's mortality to God's eternal life, breaks the grip of death over mankind and grafts us anew onto the tree of life from which God mercifully forbade us from the moment of Original Sin.

Three components of this sacrifice are critical for our purposes: first, the Mass encompasses all of time and raises it to eternity;

---

[108] Council of Trent, Session 22, chap. 1, in *The Canons and Decrees of the Council of Trent*, trans. Theodore Alois Buckley (London: George Routledge, 1851), https://www.capdox.capuchin.org.au/reform-resources-16th-century/sources/the-canons-and-decrees-of-the-council-of-trent/#post-2439-_Toc529040190.

second, the Eucharist profoundly affirms the goodness of the individual man; and third, the Mass sends us forth to labor faithfully on behalf of the Kingdom.

Liturgy and Time

The Mass is the sacrament of the Word, the perpetually renewed celebration of the Logos, made liturgically present to us in the person of the priest, the gathering of the faithful, the proclamation of the Word, and the offering of the Eucharist.[109] It is especially through these two latter elements that all of creation, extending across all of time, is raised as an offering to the Father.[110]

In the Liturgy of the Word, the faithful are led cyclically, year after year, through an encounter with the totality of time in quite a literal sense. In Genesis we not only see the beginning of time but we are also granted a glimpse of the eternity that precedes time—not temporally, of course, but causally and ontologically. And in Revelation we witness the end of time as well as that eternal liturgy into which time itself will pass away. In the beginning and in the end, we find invitations to the very life of the Trinity, which is so lovingly and heartbreakingly detailed in the remainder of the Old and New Testaments, and which gives constant witness to the Father's love of His people and His affirmation of the goodness of creation.

The modern failure to take true rest, to be properly festive in the celebration of the Lord's Day wherein we also honor the Sabbath, which God declared the first of all Israel's feasts, is in part a function of acedia's hatred of being. In particular, we recall, acedia

---

[109] Vatican Council II, Constitution on the Sacred Liturgy *Sacrosanctum Concilium* (December 4, 1963), no. 7.

[110] Ratzinger, *Spirit of the Liturgy*, 56.

elicits a keen detestation of the concrete particulars of my own existence, of the elements of being which form the context of my daily life. The Lord's Day, recalling that seventh-day rest in which God called the world "very good," and celebrating that eighth-day triumph when the fallen world witnessed Christ's victory over the Fall, puts acedia to rout when it is properly celebrated.

If the Liturgy of the Word encompasses all of time, pointing to all of history from the standpoint of eternity, then the Liturgy of the Eucharist re-presents the moment when Christ, experiencing once and for all the full weight of anxiety, embraces history entire and sacrifices Himself for its redemption. Thus, extended upon the Cross, Christ offers those who enter into His sacrifice the opportunity to make their own temporal anxiety fruitful. Mass, faithfully attended, becomes the school par excellence for that kind of presence to the eternal that St. Augustine describes as the end of human existence. Indeed, it is participation in the eternal liturgy upon which all our hope hangs. Celebrated weekly and even daily, it teaches us to live in the divine presence even in the most sorrowful or simply mundane circumstances of life. It trains us to live in that light which banishes the dismal darkness of acedia. In short, it prepares us for Heaven, granting us in time the gift of heavenly festivity so that all of our time is more and more pervaded by eternity.

Liturgy and the Goodness of Man

The effect of the Mass is not simply psychological, however. It does not simply train us to be more attentive to God's presence. Rather, through the Eucharist, the Mass unites our being with God's. At the Last Supper, Christ urged us to remain in Him as He remains in us. As usual, His words were not simply metaphorical. Or perhaps we could say they were metaphorical in the way in which only the words of the Logos can be, truly bearing the weight of their significance. In the Eucharist, Christ remains in us, so that we remain part of His Body. In our union with Him, we are likewise united with the Father, welcomed into that trinitarian love which sustains the universe in being.

As such, the Mass, in addition to affirming the goodness of the world, most profoundly affirms the goodness of the individual man. God is not content merely to look upon us and pronounce us good. His love extends as far as uniting His eternal blessedness with our meager mortality. This, too, strikes a heavy blow against acedia, which directs its weariness as much against the self as against the world. Especially in our age, so steeped in the Nietzschean and Sartrean drive for self-definition through assertion of the will, acedia whispers that we could be happy if only we could change our body, alter our gender, modify or expand our sexual preferences, and otherwise strike out against the concrete particularity of our embodiment.

Against this insidious slothful impulse to reject our own selfhood, the Eucharist rejoins the radiant, joyous *yes* of the Word Himself made flesh in a particular body at a certain point in history. The individual, in all the oddity of embodiment, in all the peculiarity, in even the tragicomedy which attends existence at each moment of time, finds his existence affirmed by the Eucharist. The enormity of this truth demands ever-renewed commitment to faithful reception of the Eucharist—reception, that is, only after proper sacramental purification by Penance. We are told in John's Gospel that it was in the moment of taking the morsel that Satan entered into Judas, and we may surmise that we face the same danger whenever we receive the Eucharist (see John 13:27). In this intimate encounter with God, whereby we are united to His Body, we are, as it were, confirmed in that disposition under which we present ourselves. ~~Receiving in sin, we seal ourselves in sin; receiving in a state of grace, we allow ourselves to be conduits to the multiplication of grace.~~ In Christ crucified, we are once more granted access to the Tree of Life. God spared Adam and Eve from eating of the Tree of Life, granting them death as a gift, that they might not eat in sin and live forever a kind of cursed half-life. How much greater the danger for us, to eat of the Bread of Life and consign ourselves to eternity amid the flames.

Liturgy and the Call to Good Work

Finally, whereas sloth makes our neighbors loathsome to us, so many obstacles to our own holiness, the Mass, by uniting us with Christ, must make us ardent laborers alongside Him in the vine-yard. How often, under the influence of sloth, are we tempted to think that we could be holy if only our children didn't constantly need our attention, or that we could truly do something good if the mundane tasks of completing our work or cleaning our homes no longer hampered us? How often are spouses, parents, and friends perceived as hindrances to the good pursuits we have envisioned for ourselves?

The Mass, as an encounter with Christ, sends us forth to preach that encounter. It demands a loving affirmation of the concrete circumstances of life and in particular of the people entrusted to our care and labor. It requires that we go forth and be about the work of each given moment, not pining for greater works or better circumstances, but freely giving the treasure of faith as a means for the leavening of society.

The liturgy, then, is the perfect antidote to acedia. Often enough, sadly, we do not experience it as such. We turn now to consider why that is: why the Mass so scarcely affects us, and why this is especially the case in our day.

Watch and Pray: The Difficulty of Liturgical Participation

With due respect to the dangers of generalization, it is likely that all Catholics know the difficulty of remaining attentive during Mass. The baby two pews in front of us, reaching over her mother's shoulder, makes every effort to catch our eye. The man behind us is coughing uncontrollably. A chance word in the homily recalls something a coworker said last week or anticipates a difficult conversation to be had tomorrow morning. Or the pastor's words rankle, whether for their political charge or their nonchalance or their heterodoxy or their orthodoxy. The stained glass is so beautiful that we find our eyes wandering everywhere but to the altar. The wood paneling is so ugly that we find our eyes shut disgustedly against it. Hunger and thirst beckon. Sleep calls so sweetly. And the kids just won't stop misbehaving. Every possible distraction is available to us in the course of a single Mass, it seems. A single hour becomes a forum for the whole chaotic gamut of human experience and imagination.

For many of us, unable to attend properly to the experience of the liturgy, the end of Mass probably brings some sense of relief. Now, we feel, our rest can begin. We can fire up the grill, crack open a beer, and kick back. We can cut the grass. We can finally grade those papers, file those reports, and prepare for the week.

Why? Why should the earthly liturgy in which the reality of eternal life with God is made present through Christ in the Eucharist leave us so unimpressed?

We may point first to those general lineaments of human existence that otherwise make it so difficult to achieve our end. As bodily beings, we are subject to all the demands of the body, with its senses, appetites, and passions. My eyes and ears can easily distract me, leading me by visible realities away from invisible ones. Hunger, thirst, and weariness demand satisfaction, making it difficult to remain watchful as the Lord undergoes His Passion. More difficult still, lust, greed, anger, and the rest of their host strive to pervert my very presence at the sacrifice, to insinuate themselves into my consciousness so that participation in the sacrifice becomes spiritual perjury.

Our intellectual capacities may likewise distract us from the reality of the Mass. We have dwelt at length on the challenges wrought by our experience of time—challenges St. Augustine discerned as lying at the root of all man's woes. Our faculties of memory and anticipation afford limitless opportunities for being drawn out of Mass, often in a form of anxiety. We fear the results of the test we took on Friday. We have a presentation to give Monday morning and haven't yet adequately prepared. Or, more positively but little less distractingly, we have an engagement with friends in the afternoon, or reservations at a fine restaurant, or a chance at last to take the boat out on the lake for some fishing. In the very liturgical space where the entirety of time is presented to us and lifted to eternity, our own limited experience of time frequently draws us out of the eternal.

Such are the intransigent features of human nature, the challenges of being ensouled bodies who in every age struggle to direct our attention to the eternal now, which is always reaching out to us in love. To this must be added certain features of modern life which have made such attention even more difficult. We wish here to emphasize three: the rapid advance of technology, the loss of symbolic imagination, and the development of a modern economy which repudiates festivity.

There is perhaps no more potent enemy of presence to our immediate surroundings and especially to the things of eternity than the smartphone. While precise figures vary, data suggests that average smartphone users spend no fewer than 3½ hours daily on their phones. In comparison to the amount of time spent in prayer, especially in Lord's Day worship, the figure is troubling. It becomes more so when we consider that this amounts to just over one day out of seven devoted to our phones. As a culture, that is, we offer a weekly Sabbath to our phones rather than to our God.

Moreover, smartphones exacerbate our tendencies to be drawn out of the present by opening, as it were, the totality of the world to our perusal. In the midst of life's ordinary circumstances, of sending an e-mail for work, of bathing children, of cooking dinner, my smartphone beckons me to ignore my colleagues, my daughters, my wife, in favor of examining the political situation in East Africa or the development of the latest Taylor Swift album or the troubling weather patterns in the South China Sea. These same temptations arise during Mass. And though smartphones make for easy pocket missals, their usage during the liturgy may present a near occasion of distraction. Nothing is easier than to swipe over from iBreviary to Facebook and scroll my way through the remainder of the homily.

The technological thrust of modern life, with its scientist underpinnings, has also played a critical role in wearing away our symbolic imaginations. We have called the Mass the sacrament of the Word. As technology advances (toward what? Caldecott rightly asks),[111] our own intellectual capacities, which can be said to hinge on our capacity for language, are frequently weakened. With Google always in our pockets, we feel no need to remember much of anything. With Netflix available to occupy every moment of boredom, we allow our imaginations to atrophy, handing over to the filmmakers and series producers our own capacity for creative

[111] Caldecott, *Not as the World Gives*, 84.

engagement with words and ideas. No longer do we hold a book in our hands and let the words take shape under the magical lantern light of the imagination. No longer do a friend's words in conversation call forth, as if from the depths of the soul, a line of Homer or Keats.

Indeed, our very use of words has become impoverished. Bleached as if by the backlight of our smartphone screens, our texted, tweeted words all too often bleed out to a state just above meaninglessness. Our use of language has become more and more utilitarian, more commercial, and, critically, more scientistic. That is, we tend to reduce our linguistic transactions to causal phenomena of the same type as those which science studies.

As Walker Percy is careful to point out, though, man's use of language extends far beyond the level of mere dyadic causal chains. We do not simply utter sounds to satisfy instinctual drives, in the way that an infant cries for relief from some discomfort or a chimpanzee signs for a banana. Instead, man's linguistic capacities are triadic; that is, they always involve the word itself, the word's object of reference, and the concept. For instance, the word *elephant* is one thing. An actual elephant is another. And there is also a concept, *elephant*, which we develop in our minds through many instances of experiencing elephants. It is our very ability to use language thus which allows us to tell stories. How astonishing to imagine the moment when man first became aware of this capacity, when, gathered around the campfire, he could begin to tell stories of the elk rather than simply to use the vocable for elk to indicate the presence of an elk. This breaking through into the daylight of language, this capacity for sharing in the creative use of the Logos, is what most fundamentally separates us from the animals.[112]

---

[112] Percy, *Message in the Bottle*, 31.

Words are nothing less than opportunities for us to participate in the life of the Word, and nowhere is that more so than in the Mass, whose words and gestures constantly refer us to an extratemporal order of being which it belongs to our symbolic imaginations to recognize. In seeing a priest process up the length of the nave at the beginning of Mass and ascend the steps of the altar, I should see not only the physical process at hand but also the historical incident of Christ's entry into Jerusalem and ascent to the altar of the Cross, not to mention the entry of the ancient priests of Israel into the holy of holies. When I hear the words "Holy, holy, holy," I should hear not only the voices of the priest and the people around me but also the song of the angels attending the throne of God, eternally offering this song of praise which, through the mediation of Christ, becomes a feast to which the members of His Body are present even within time. Such capacities have rather rapidly eroded under the influence of technologically driven scientism, which reduces not only the material world but also man himself to the level of mechanically explainable phenomena. We have become a world of literalists, much to the detriment of our ability to be festive.[113]

The third, less outwardly noticeable but therefore all the more insidious facet of modern life that makes authentic liturgical celebration so difficult concerns our culture's abnegation of true

---

[113] Closely related to festivity in its liturgical context is the notion of play. Play, as Johan Huizinga notes, "goes beyond the confines of purely physical or purely biological activity. It is a *significant* function.... In play there is something 'at play' which transcends the immediate needs of life and imparts meaning to the action." Johan Huizinga, *Homo Ludens: A Study of the Play Element in Culture* (1950; repr., Boston: Beacon Press, 1970), 1. The modern scientistic milieu can make little sense of play or festivity.

festivity. It is critical that we specify *true* festivity, because our culture has neither lost the yearning for festivity nor abandoned attempts at festivity. The day of this writing is, I find, not merely the twenty-first of October, but also National Pumpkin Cheesecake Day, not to mention National Mammography Day, National Witch Hazel Day, National Reptile Awareness Day, and Back to the Future Day. The multiplication of such days is overlaid with a tireless prolongation of the secularized holidays of autumn and winter. Halloween decorations begin to sprout in neighbors' yards in early September. By October, the department stores have already begun to set out Christmas décor. On the one hand, we might do worse than to view such "holiday spirit" as evidence that our culture is not, and never can be, lost entirely. It belongs to man to crave the holy, and while our modern methods of seeking holiness are puerile in the extreme, they nonetheless speak to a good craving. We long for the joyful moment of festivity in which we taste something of the divine life. And we attempt, by spreading our festivity across an ever-longer season, to approximate something of that eternal festivity to which we are called in Heaven. We see a version of this, on a smaller scale, perhaps, in the distension of the football week, from the main Sunday celebration to Monday and Thursday night games, with constant commentary and speculation in between. We see a far grander version of this impulse in the calendar of the saints, according to whose perspective every day is, rightly speaking, a feast.

However, such attempts at festivity as our commercial Halloween-Christmas corridor and our daily multiplication of feasts fail to recognize certain key components of authentic festivity.

In the first place, our commercialized celebrations have lost a true sense of sacrifice. True festivity always involves such sacrifice, whether of a cereal or animal offering, as in the great festivals of ancient Israel, or simply of time and profit. (We will see that degrees of festivity and degrees of sacrifice are, indeed, directly proportional to each other.) For the ancients, celebration of the winter solstice involved precisely a waste of that abundance upon which survival till spring depended. Israel's ancient feasts involved the loss of grain and animals but also the loss of time in Sabbath rest. In the Jubilee years, it meant also loss of the profits of debts to be paid.

We struggle so gravely to celebrate the Lord's Day, in part, then, because we have lost the capacity for joyous, life-giving waste. We will not close the shop and sacrifice a day's profit. We will not attend Mass and sacrifice an hour's work. Often enough, we do not waste because we feel we cannot waste. Our economy depends so far on our indebtedness, and the weight of our debts looms so large in all our considerations, that time spent in worship and contemplation seems an extravagance we simply can't afford.[114] Our culture, having made limitless monetary growth its god, could be said to have cut itself off categorically from the kind of sacrifice which makes for true worship.

In his *Theory of Religion*, Georges Bataille makes the case that cultural value is always tied to waste.[115] That is, we can tell what a society values by observing the ways it is willing to waste, to spend, its substance. In the Gospel, for instance, Mary, breaking the jar of aromatic nard and anointing Jesus' body, gives a prime example of such "waste" (and it does indeed seem a waste to Judas). Likewise, the medieval world left us immense visions of extravagance in the service of the divine in its cathedrals, whose construction

---

[114] Caldecott, *Not as the World Gives*, 72–74.
[115] Georges Bataille, *Theory of Religion*, trans. Robert Hurley (New York: Zone Books, 1989), 43–61.

involved the giving over, the sacrifice, of countless artisans' and laborers' lifetimes.

Where do we waste? Consider the example of Louisiana State University football. The Tigers' present head coach, Brian Kelly, collects a salary of nine million dollars. Just yesterday, as of this writing, he received a $500,000 bonus for leading the team to bowl eligibility, a threshold the team is almost guaranteed to clear in any given year. In contrast, for many Catholic parishes, $500,000 may represent an entire year's budget.[116] Monetarily, as a culture, we make our priorities plain. Neither authentic worship nor the more dubious liturgy of Tiger Stadium finds its primary purpose in any practical utility. For this reason, the degree to which we devote ourselves and our substance to them indicates our priorities.

Time, too, forms a critical component of our substance, and again, the use of our time paints a compelling picture of our own cultural values. How do we spend the time given to us each Sunday?

We are inclined to waste according to what we value. And this notion of value points to another component of festivity which has been lost on the religion of our age. That is, people can only be festive where they feel the source of festivity has true bearing on their lives.[117] If, as a culture, we have abandoned Lord's Day worship in favor of any number of secular forms of entertainment, distraction, or relaxation, it is because the liturgy no longer seems to most people to have any relevance to the actual business of living in the modern world.

Why is this the case? To a large degree, the answer can be found in those same factors which have given sloth such ample

---

[116] See studies by the Center for Applied Research in the Apostolate and Villanova's Center for the Study of Church Management.

[117] Pieper, *In Tune with the World*, 26.

opportunities. Our true end in contemplative worship of God has come to seem an abstract artifact of a bygone age, banished by the sober lights of scientific reason, technological expansion, and limitless economic growth. With ourselves as gods, and the only will to be followed our own through the exercise of ever-greater financial means, true abandonment to God and His providence is the sort of "waste," of commitment of self, which we no longer value nor care to cultivate.

How, then, to re-establish a proper understanding of man's end and thus to restore to man a sense of the supreme relevance of liturgy? This was one of the fundamental questions of the Second Vatican Council, yet it is on this precise score that the council is utterly dismissed by some and, even by its proponents, closely scrutinized. We turn now to this crux of the modern crisis of faith, the ascendancy of sloth, and the rejection of the Lord's Day.

Sacrosanctum Concilium[118]

Of the many disputations current within the districts of Mother Church, there is probably none so pressing, or so divisive, as that concerning the Second Vatican Council. We need not look far, especially on the Internet, to find examples of the most extreme naïveté and the most intense pessimism in commentators' assessments of the council. There are those, on the one hand, who proclaim that the Church has entered a new golden age of tolerance and liturgical vigor since its conclusion. There are likewise

---

[118] The Constitution on the Sacred Liturgy, promulgated by Pope Paul VI on December 4, 1963, sought to reform and promote the liturgy. The difference between what this constitution recommends and what has occurred in liturgical practice constitutes some of the richest ground for continued reform and growth in the life of the Church.

those who would have us believe that practically all of the Church's present problems have followed directly on the council. And there are those who, like Pope Benedict XVI did, take a more measured approach, appealing to the frequent radiance of the texts of Vatican II, a radiance heavily founded on Scripture, the Fathers, and the Council of Trent, while also recognizing and deploring the missteps taken by many in the years since the council.

This raging debate frequently descends into a cruel debauch of incendiary language, ad hominem attacks, and, it might be said, flirtation with despair. Judging from many commentators' views on the present state of Catholic affairs, it would seem that the Holy Spirit is no longer at work in guiding the Church. If that were the case, quite simply, there would be no Church.

Pope Benedict XVI, in his first address as pope to the Roman Curia at Christmas, famously spoke of the two hermeneutics, or principles of interpretation, in the wake of the council. On the one hand, in keeping with the so-called "spirit of Vatican II," there arose a "hermeneutic of rupture," an interpretive lens which saw the actual council documents as concessions to traditional decorum. These documents, nonetheless, were not binding in their turn to tradition and, by their frequent inconclusiveness, provided the Modernist element in the Church, which was no doubt present at the council and remains powerful to our day, with an opportunity to make its long-sought alterations. On the other hand, we should seek, Pope Benedict thought, a "hermeneutic of reform," one which, reading the documents in good faith and in light of the tradition to which they so frequently referred, sought always the deepening of liturgical understanding and hence of the Church's mission in the world.

In our day, there has arisen a third hermeneutic, one I would call a hermeneutic of suspicion. Its adherents have a tendency to read all of the institutional Church's actions since Vatican II in the worst possible light.

We should at all times seek to root out error, going with Aristotle in loving the truth even more than we love our friends. We should be zealous for the Lord in our waking and in our sleeping and especially in our worship. Yet if our zeal would be fruitful, it must go always with Christ. We must, as St. John Henry Newman preached, walk in sunshine even when we sorrow, whether that sorrow be over the state of our culture or our Church. The slothful temptation to give in to disgust with our circumstances is perhaps nowhere more persistent than in our understanding of our own Church.

We must, if we are to avoid sloth and inspire faith, turn God's seventh-day eye upon the world, speaking the deep-down goodness of things.[119] We must not turn all things to the bad, as the evil one does. We must not give the worst possible reading to all events and actions. We must, finally, recall that the Church is not simply her hierarchical structure but is the living Body of Christ of which we, the laity, make up the vast majority, and if we feel the hierarchical Church has failed in much of what she owes to us, we should also search keenly into our own hearts after the ways we have failed her.[120] Above all, we must seek transformative encounter with Christ so that we, like Peter after the Resurrection and Pentecost, might truly possess the inheritance of faith, so that, as American Catholics, our gift to posterity will not be silver or gold but true healing in the name of Jesus Christ the Nazorean (see Acts 3:6).

---

[119] See the poem by Gerard Manley Hopkins, "God's Grandeur," available at Poetry Foundation, https://www.poetryfoundation. org/poems/44395/gods-grandeur.

[120] See Hans Urs von Balthasar, *Engagement with God: The Drama of Christian Discipleship*, trans. R. John Halliburton (San Francisco, Ignatius Press, 2008).

Our consideration of the council must here remain quite limited, concerning itself primarily with (1) the ways in which the errors since the council have resulted in the exacerbation of our modern tendency toward acedia and the resultant abandonment of the Lord's Day, and (2) the respects in which the actual documents of the council, reflective as they are of the very concern of this book, can serve as guides to the restoration of true worship and true festivity.

Nonetheless, our inquiry may be aided by a brief survey of the historical context which led up to the council and which has likewise prompted this book.

In parsing out the roots of modern anti-festivity, and Vatican II's attempts to combat them, we are brought inevitably to the French Revolution. Not only did the reign of Robespierre look to overthrow Catholicism as the heart of French patrimony, but it also, as Pieper vividly relates, sought to establish its own, often quite astonishing, festivals of reason.[121] These were great public occasions, their greatness only partially diminished by their coercive character, wherein citizens were effectively ordered out of their homes and given prearranged roles in the enactment of these reasonable feasts. It is perhaps difficult, in our age, when we so little celebrate great artists and thinkers, to imagine the grandeur which attended a festival arranged by Jacques-Louis David, with Robespierre as chief celebrant at the feast of St. Voltaire; to picture a day devoted to hacking away at papier-mâché reconstructions of the Bastille in order to release the noble child reason trapped within; to imagine drinking from the breasts of a great statue of imagination. It is disturbing to hear of the apotheosis of St. Voltaire, at which the congregants sang a parody

[121] Pieper, *In Tune with the World*, 45ff.

of "O Salutaris Hostia." These new liturgies were intended to replace the Mass as the ultimate touchpoint of liberty, equality, and fraternity, bringing men and women together on the common ground of the intellect, safe from the cruel discriminations of king and God.

The revolution, with its seizure of Church lands and gutting of cathedrals, and with broad popular anti-Catholic sentiment at its back, ultimately paved the way for a new European Modernism in which the Church was firmly separated from the state, leading the Church to close ranks, at least on some level, and to withdraw from the modern world.

Now, it bears noting that the revitalization of the Church has always demanded withdrawal, for a time, from public affairs. Christ Himself withdrew to the mountaintops for silent prayer and invited His disciples to come away for a while to be nourished for their ministry. The reinvigoration of the Church by St. Benedict hinged on his own withdrawal from the noise, both physical and spiritual, of Rome. Yet such withdrawal, seeking deeper union with the Trinity, entails a subsequent return to society for the sake of its sanctification.[122]

Put in the simplest terms, much of the history of the Church in the modern world can be construed as a withdrawal from the Modernist Reign of Terror, a withdrawal which involved the key moment of the forfeiture of the Papal States, and a subsequent return to the world spurred in part by the concerns of the Liturgical Movement and the *Nouvelle Théologie*. The latter were concerned with restoring the celebrated noble simplicity of the Tridentine Mass and re-emphasizing the radiance of Scripture and the Fathers, as well as with removing liturgical and Scholastic incrustations which made the life of the Church, at least according to some

---

[122] Brumfield, *Benedict Proposal*, 4

witnesses, less available to the faithful and less open to the rest of the world.

Such a reading is, again, quite simple. Yet it may be helpful in understanding certain facts which must be answered if we are to place the blame for our current predicament squarely at the feet of Vatican II.

We see, for example, that the downward trend in Mass attendance in America begins not with the convocation of the council nor with its conclusion, but substantially earlier, in 1955.[123] And this downward slide, troubling as it is, particularly for those of us who live in the West, should also be read against the fact that, by some measures, Catholicism has in the last century enjoyed the largest growth in its history, with the worldwide number of Catholics rising from 267 million in 1900 to 1.36 billion today, with 16 million Catholics entering the Church in 2020.[124]

Here we would do well to ponder the words of Gervase Crouchback, the saintly father of Evelyn Waugh's *Sword of Honor* trilogy, who reminds his son Guy, himself beset by sloth, that in matters of the faith "quantitative judgments don't apply."[125] Crouchback's language is strong, and if we take it too literally, we might miss the point: in the spiritual life, the only true measure is love. Hence the Good Shepherd leaves ninety-nine in the desert to seek one, a spiritual calculus which makes no sense according to worldly reckoning. Then, too, if we suppose that authentic revelation of

---

[123] Lydia Saad, "Catholics' Church Attendance."

[124] Rev. Dorian Llywelyn, S.J., "Global Christianity: The Future of the Catholic Church," Institute for Advanced Catholic Studies at USC, April 30, 2022, https://dornsife.usc.edu/iacs/2022/04/30/global-christianity/.

[125] Evelyn Waugh, *Sword of Honor:* (New York: Back Bay Books, 2012), 522–523.

God's Word will necessarily lead to quantitative increase in the Church, we have only to look at Scripture to see that in the critical moments of revelation, the active body of Christ's followers almost always becomes smaller. When Christ calls Himself the Bread of Life, for instance, the great crowds leave him, as do almost all His followers. And when Christ is arrested and later crucified, only one of His apostles is there. There is today much talk of sedevacantism—the possibility that there is no valid pope. Yet perhaps we could say that the see was never more vacant than when Peter was not there at the foot of the Cross. Nonetheless, the Church persists.

Likewise, if we think that, prior to the council, there was no impetus within the Church for liturgical reform, or that such liturgical reform was prima facie opposed to continuity with the Council of Trent and the rest of Catholic Tradition, we come up against the insights of the Liturgical Movement, which saw that, as Pope Benedict put it, the development of liturgy had become like something of a translucent whitewash over the celebration itself, protecting it, certainly, but also not permitting it to breathe and to shine forth in its overmastering beauty.

Then, too, there exists a notion that, whereas previous ecumenical councils had been summoned together to respond to specific crises, the Second Vatican Council was summoned for no reason, or merely as a pretext for introducing Modernism. While we cannot deny the influence of Modernism in the subsequent life of the Western Church, we also should remain cognizant of the fact that the council was convened in the aftermath of the bloodiest conflicts in history, conflicts in which Christian warred against Christian—in an era when rational enlightenment and scientific progress had apparently brought man to the brink of a new era of unprecedented peace and prosperity.

How, then, had the Western world, that is, the world nourished on classicalism and Christianity, so desperately failed? The council, I take it, was convened with such questions in mind, and with an eye to restoring the Church as the true ship of humanity and the lodestar of her navigation. Let us look, then, into the ways in which the council has failed to achieve this goal, and also into the ways in which her documents may still provide light for our way forward.

You Shall Become Like Gods: The Logos and the Dialogical

When Christ entrusted the Church to St. Peter, he assured the fisherman that the gates of Hell would not prevail against the humble and glorious Bark upon which we sail to our salvation (Matt. 16:18). For many of us, it feels as though the gates of the Church are hard-pressed to hold up under the advance of Satan's armies, yet the paradigm set before us in Christ's commission of Peter is one in which the Church herself marches against Satan, whose dark kingdom will not, in the end, be able to resist. This does not mean that the Church will march forth in pomp, with the grandeur of Soviet or Nazi military displays. Rather, to borrow from Tolkien, perhaps the Church, sheltering in a Gondor which is a shadow of her former glory, will weather the fiercest of the enemy's attacks and then send forth a meager band which can hardly muster the feeling of hope in its breast but which hopes all the same in the promise of the Lord: This is the day that I have made. Rejoice, and be glad.

Between the extremes of contemplative withdrawal from society and apocalyptic battle with Hell, we are certainly called to engagement with the world, seeking to spread the Kingdom as the King has commanded. We are each, like Adam, called to till and cultivate the garden entrusted to our care. Yet there are forces which would see the garden laid waste or, best of all, see the cultivators expelled. Such was the influence of the serpent whose questioning led to our Fall. And the process of that Fall, the sly insinuations of the dragon and then Adam and Eve's ineffectual response, may provide guidance for a Church which seeks to engage the world in which she is present yet not at home.[126]

The serpent begins with a question: "Did God really say, 'You shall not eat from any of the trees in the garden'?" (Gen. 3:1). Satan, expert provocateur, begins by exaggerating the scope of the limitation God has placed on Adam and Eve. Curiously, Eve responds in kind, though to a lesser degree, saying, "We may eat of the fruit of the trees in the garden; it is only about the fruit of the tree in the middle of the garden that God said, 'You shall not eat it or even touch it, or else you will die'" (Gen. 3:2–3). It seems an innocent enough answer, and indeed, Eve's reply may simply constitute plain inference from God's command not to eat of the tree. After all, that which we ought not eat is best left untouched as well. But the fact is that God did not say anything about not *touching* the tree of knowledge of good and evil. Eve, confronted by the serpent's putting words in God's mouth, does the same thing. Is it possible that Eve, dialoguing with the serpent, has already begun to become like the serpent? Could it be that her relation of God's command indicates some questioning of the command that has already taken place in her heart? In walking with God in the cool of the day, did her questions ever linger on her lips, only to be withheld and given later in conference with the serpent?

Whatever the content of Eve's heart and the shades of meaning attributable to her response, her way of being in the world shifts rapidly from corresponding to God's vision of things to reflecting

[126] *Sacrosanctum Concilium*, no. 2.

the serpent's. She looks at the fruit and sees that it is good, though not good in the manner of God's pronouncement of goodness upon the created world. It is not simply good but now rather good *for* various uses, whether nourishment or enlightenment. The three kinds of goodness Eve sees in the fruit—facets of good which may be likened to the threefold concupiscence against which St. John warns us—lead her in a startling way to become *not* like God, as the serpent had promised. Indeed, drawn from the side of Adam, fashioned in love according to God's image, after His likeness, Eve already possesses the likeness the serpent offers. What happens, though, when she eats? Immediately her eyes are opened. It is a simple consequence, and one we could expect as a result of the acquisition of knowledge, to which Aristotle so closely allies the faculty of sight.[127] But the biblical author is leading us to a more radical understanding of what has happened to Eve. In becoming aware of good and evil, she becomes not like God but like the serpent, which has no eyelids and thus always goes about with its eyes open. Eve, falling victim to acedia, allows her own proper end—life with God—to become hateful to her.

Here lies a clue, perhaps, to the proper means for dialoguing with a culture inimical to faith, or at least an example of the improper means. Dialogue with the serpent, discussion of the laws of God with God's enemy rather than first with God Himself, leads almost inevitably, by way of our concupiscence, to our becoming one with the evil one who plays interlocutor.

Of the more measured criticisms of Vatican II, the one which is perhaps most cogent with respect to the council itself and which identifies how the council could be said to have opened the way for its injurious aftereffects, points to its apparently overly optimistic

---

[127] Aristotle, *Metaphysics*, bk. 1, sec. 980a

assessment of the possibilities for the modern world's conversion. Especially in *Gaudium et Spes*, Ratzinger and many like-minded theologians recognized an openness to the modern world that did not adequately account for the need of conviction upon the Cross.[128]

Again, the council documents as a rule—especially *Sacrosanctum Concilium*, itself the fruit not so much of the immediate moment but of a century of development on the part of the Liturgical Movement—looked most urgently to transmission of the Catholic Faith entire to the modern world. As Pope John XXIII put it, "The greatest concern of the Ecumenical Council is this, that the sacred deposit of Christian doctrine should be more effectively defended and presented."[129]

Christendom had failed, and its failure had slid from the colossal tremors of the French Revolution to the unspeakable horrors of the world wars. The question of the council, then, was how the light of the Christian faith could be made to illuminate the modern darkness. The forceful denunciations of modernity, the posture of radical rejection which marked the nineteenth century, had evidently done little to forestall modernity's advance.[130] New

---

[128] See Brumfield, *Benedict Proposal*, 43ff.

[129] Pope John XXIII, "Opening Address to the Council," October 11, 1962, quoted in Peter M. J. Stravinskas, "On Pope John XXIII's Opening Address at the Second Vatican Council," *Catholic World Report*, October 11, 2022, https://www.catholicworldreport.com /2022/10/11/on-pope-john-xxiiis-opening-address-at-the-second-vatican-council/.

[130] See Pope Benedict XVI, "Address of his Holiness Benedict XVI to the Roman Curia Offering Them His Christmas Greetings," December 22, 2005, https://www.vatican.va/content/benedict-xvi/en/speeches/2005/december/documents/hf_ben_xvi_spe _20051222_roman-curia.html.

methods of dialogue, enriched by the example of Christ's own dialogue with the culture into which He was born, were needed.

In the Gospels, however, we note that Jesus does not allow Himself to fall into the pattern of questioning and speculation that had marked Eve's talk with the serpent. Tempted by Satan in the desert, Christ responds with direct quotations from Scripture, putting no words in God's mouth but rather becoming, as indeed He was, a mouthpiece for the proclamation of the Word. Similarly, when questioned by the Pharisees and Sadducees in a spirit of deception, Christ Himself becomes the questioner.

The Church in the modern world is constantly under interrogation of the sort the devil employed with Eve. We hear shouted, in serpentine accents: Did God really say homosexuality is a sin? Did God really say you should not have sex outside marriage? Did God really tell you not to use contraception? In a world which has, through acedia, become hateful to itself, in which men hate themselves and see mankind as the principal scourge on the earth, one of the few supposed cures for our self-loathing has become a search for unique identity, apart from any end, apart from any will superior to our own. This will is most easily, and pleasurably, asserted under the species of sexual expression. And so we notice that a great deal of modernity's questioning of the Church swirls around notions of sex and identity. But at the heart of these questions always lurks acedia's self-loathing: Did God really say that He loves you? Did God really create you out of infinite love? Did God really die for your sins on a cross? Did God really offer you happiness in Paradise? Surely, we hateful men could never merit such divine largesse. And indeed, modernity is right: we could not merit this. All the more should we rejoice in it.

But such rejoicing cannot be allowed to wander beyond the precincts of the Cross, the joy of which can never be separated from sacrificial love and from our own penitent offerings of self for conversion. Rejoicing loosed from the Cross is swiftly emptied of its joy, and much of the rejoicing that followed in the wake of the council quickly fell under the spell of modernity. The so-called spirit of Vatican II, turning to modernity without keeping ear and heart directed to the Lord, opened the way for a wan Catholicism, which became little different from its cultural surroundings, becoming in many places a meager attempt to emulate the kind of festive unity that was, at the time, to be found in Beatles concerts and sporting events.

The result has been moral confusion and the frightening multiplication of suburban churches which, architecturally, take their cues more from Pizza Hut than from St. Peter's—and offer choruses more suited to the smallest offstage gathering of musicians at a third-rate neighborhood music festival than to the eternal praises of the saints and angels. Anthony Esolen gives keen expression to the often-ironic process of this desacralization at his home church of St. Thomas Aquinas: "Most of the ceiling survived, but Peter and Paul disappeared, leaving the church in the absurd position of commemorating the Ten Apostles, bereft of their chief and of the great apostle to the Gentiles. The delicate background was painted over in icy white. The marble communion rail and the great altar met the jackhammer. The organ in the loft was removed, and no one knows in what landfill its hundred pipes have been crushed."[131]

Observing such a state of affairs, even apart from the manifold ethical confusions rampant in our day, it is tempting to wash our hands of the council. Yet we might find some ersatz comfort in

---

[131] Anthony Esolen, *Real Music: A Guide to the Timeless Hymns of the Church* (Charlotte, NC: Tan Books, 2016), xii.

the words of St. Basil after the Council of Nicaea, words which could well be applied to our own day.

> But when the attitude of our foes against us was changed from one of long standing and bitter strife to one of open warfare, then, as is well known, the war was split up in more ways than I can tell into many subdivisions, so that all men were stirred to a state of inveterate hatred alike by common party spirit and individual suspicion. But what storm at sea was ever so fierce and wild as this tempest of the Churches? In it every landmark of the Fathers has been moved; every foundation, every bulwark of opinion has been shaken: everything buoyed up on the unsound is dashed about and shaken down. We attack one another. We are overthrown by one another. If our enemy is not the first to strike us, we are wounded by the comrade at our side. If a foeman is stricken and falls, his fellow soldier tramples him down. There is at least this bond of union between us that we hate our common foes, but no sooner have the enemy gone by than we find enemies in one another. And who could make a complete list of all the wrecks?[132]

As Nicaea nonetheless became a cornerstone of the future development of Christian life, so, too, we might hope for the Second Vatican Council to become a guide to our journey through the third millennium. We might read *Sacrosanctum Concilium* thus: as a keen light cast over our tradition, whereby we might see in that tradition the great riches which mother Church always presents to us for the journey onward.

---

[132] St. Basil, *De Spiritu Sancto*, chap. 30, no. 77.

Restoring the Liturgy

The Second Vatican Council stated quite plainly its intention to restore the liturgy to its proper place in the Christian life, seeking to send forth the Body of Christ in a more effective mission, adding to that Body and enabling a greater number of souls to enjoy a foretaste of life in the heavenly Jerusalem. However, its efforts have as yet not stopped the decline of Catholic life in the West. Instead, Western Catholicism has been marked by increased moral confusion and decreased liturgical participation—which, most sadly of all, all-too-often includes the abuse of the Mass itself. These two markings go hand in hand, with modernist confusion about the nature of reality and about the end of human life leading to both moral turpitude and the ossification of the Mass as a wooden relic of a bygone era, an event in which modern man could hardly begin to actively, festively participate. The results must always be alarming. As Pope St. Pius X admonishes, "It is vain to hope that the blessing of heaven will descend abundantly upon us, when our homage to the Most High, instead of ascending in the odor of sweetness, puts into the hand of the Lord the scourges wherewith of old the Divine Redeemer drove the unworthy profaners from the Temple."[133]

Yet it was precisely active participation on the part of the people to which the council, especially as laid out in *Sacrosanctum Concilium*, aspired. We consider briefly, now, what the document understood by active participation. This shall lead in subsequent chapters to a study of how architecture, music, silence, and personal

---

[133] Pope Pius X, Letter to the Cardinal Vicar of Rome on Sacred Music *Tra le Sollecitudini* (December 8, 1903), introduction, Papal Encyclicals Online, https://www.papalencyclicals.net/pius10/tra-le-sollecitudini.htm.

prayer are the means by which the liturgy may be restored in light of *Sacrosanctum Concilium.*

"In the earthly liturgy we take part in a foretaste of that heavenly liturgy which is celebrated in the holy city of Jerusalem toward which we journey as pilgrims, where Christ is sitting at the right hand of God, a minister of the holy of holies and of the true tabernacle."[134] The Mass, that is, elevates us within time to a vision of the eternal, shedding the light of the eighth day, the re-creation of all things upon time, through which we journey as pilgrims It ushers us into the presence of the Trinity, where Christ ministers, most fully revealing man to man himself.[135]

In the Mass, that is, we experience the goal of human existence. As such, "Mother Church earnestly desires that all the faithful should be led to that fully conscious, and active participation in liturgical celebrations which is demanded by the very nature of the liturgy."[136] We tend to think of active participation as consisting of outward acts such as responses and gestures, or duties such as lectoring and cantoring.[137] Yet the use of the term *active participation*, which dates back to Pope St. Pius X's *Tra le Sollecitudini* (1903), should be most properly associated with bodily participation in the life and sacrifice of Christ in the Eucharist. Indeed, Pope St. Pius X, though his motu proprio dealt with liturgical music, is the patron saint of First Communicants, for his lowering the age of First Communion.

Sacrosanctum Concilium sets forth several ways in which Christ is present in the liturgy, ways in which the people, as the body,

[134] *Sacrosanctum Concilium*, no. 8.

[135] See Vatican Council II, Pastoral Constitution on the Church in the Modern World *Gaudium et Spes* (December 7, 1965), no. 22 — a passage frequently cited by Pope John Paul II.

[136] *Sacrosanctum Concilium*, no. 14.

[137] Ratzinger, *Spirit of the Liturgy*, 80.

are called to participate. First, He is present in the person of the ordained minister. Second, and most especially, He is present in the Eucharist. He is present, third, in His Word, and fourth, in the people. The order of priority is clear. It is through the Eucharist that Christ is most fully and effectively present in the Mass, and it is through the Eucharist that the Word is fulfilled, that the priest participates in the ministry of Christ, and that the people are made one body.

Hence, though it is true that the Mass is a communal meal, active participation in that meal does not refer simply to loving attention to our neighbors. The meal that Christ bid us remember was not concluded in the Upper Room but only on the Cross, where the last bitter cup was drunk. Active participation consists in placing ourselves upon the altar with the Lamb. It is in this sacrifice, whereby we have the opportunity to fill up "what is lacking in the afflictions of Christ" (Col. 1:24), that the Eucharist makes the Church. In it alone are we made strong for the journey, made capable of going forth with the eyes of Christ crucified, who gazes down upon His beloved disciple, who had just partaken of the Lord's flesh, and upon His beloved mother, through whom the Lord had received His flesh.

Restoration of the liturgy is always a matter of restoration of the Eucharist, the sacrament upon which the glory of the heavenly Jerusalem is built and around which the angelic choirs lift up their songs of praise. Vatican II, seeking to combat the decline in Church life after the world wars, sought precisely such restoration of active participation through fitting celebration of the Eucharist. Sadly, we have only to open our eyes and ears to the reality of many suburban American churches to see that these efforts, weakened by poor Church leadership in the decades after the council, have as yet borne little fruit. Nonetheless, we must continue to celebrate what is good in the council, and look to it and the rest of the Catholic tradition for guidance in the third millennium. Our efforts at reform, at restoration of the Lord's Day, must look to the means whereby through our senses, through space and time, we may be guided back to that flesh which is true food and that blood which is true drink. We thus turn our attention to sacred art, architecture, and music, looking to *Sacrosanctum Concilium* and the tradition on which it draws to see the ways in which these arts might help to shape our eucharistic faith.

5

Sacred Space: Liturgy, Art, and Architecture

It belongs to man to delight in belonging. Our restlessness craves surcease in the peace of being present to another and so finally becoming at home with ourselves. Only in Christ do we find the peace of our proper place, the eternal place from which all passing realities flow, the space of love at the heart of the Trinity.

Our age is one of special restlessness. While Americans are on the whole less migratory than half a century ago, mobility is becoming increasingly possible as technology allows greater work flexibility and opens constant windows into the many corners of the world. Social media in particular has a way of showing us the beauties of other countries, states, and communities, such that we can very easily grow frustrated with the dull, grim reality of our own jobs, our own families, our own cities. The world beckons, and sloth wonders if we wouldn't be better off out there, in a place where our talents and time could finally be fulfilled.

The place we all seek, the one that looms beyond all visions of the perfect earthly community, is the heavenly Jerusalem. And, thanks be to God, Catholic churches around the world offer portals to that heavenly realm, temples where the Lamb who was slain lives within golden tabernacles, softly burning with the light of candle flame. In the liturgy, we are offered a taste of the joy that awaits us at our journey's end, and the churches where we worship carve out a space dedicated to that joy.

It is proper, then, that our places of worship be constructed for such joy, with reverence for the supreme sacrifice on which the heavenly Jerusalem is founded and with the utmost effort to glorify the God who wishes us to share His joy. Unfortunately, many of us, particularly in America, find ourselves worshipping in spaces little reflective of liturgical reality and thus little suited to drawing us into that reality.

A full liturgical aesthetics lies far beyond the scope of the present work. However, we might gain ground toward our aim of restoring the Lord's Day by considering how good architecture reveals reality and helps us to overcome sloth by transforming our experience of time.

Our investigations will be aided by a brief survey, first of the history of Israel's temple worship, then of Jesus' transformation of that worship, and finally the development of church architecture. This investigation should indicate that while there is no one style of architecture which is normative, there are certain principles which should govern not only our construction and decoration but also our placement of churches.

Prior to Moses, the establishment of sacred places was already a critical component of God's growing intimacy with Abraham, Isaac, and Jacob. Even as early as the Creation narrative, we find God fashioning a world that itself had all the features of a temple: a space set apart for the glory of the Lord and for man's participation in that glory. When man failed in his role, and God had decided to wipe the earth clean, He nonetheless commanded Noah to build an ark which would itself become a cosmos, riding out the storm of un-becoming. Much later, the ancient patriarchs, as we have seen, frequently established altars in commemoration of their encounters with God. The sentiment behind these establishments is most beautifully expressed in Jacob's words at Bethel, words which the Christian would do well to realize everywhere he goes: "Truly, the LORD is in this place.... This is nothing else but the house of God" (Gen. 28:16-17).

The fervor that moved the patriarchs to establish these places was ritualized when Israel encountered the Lord at Sinai, where God gave Moses not only the Commandments but also His detailed instructions for the tabernacle that would house the Ark of the Covenant and function as a portable Sinai, a sacred space which the Lord would fill so that in all their journeys the people could be reminded of the reason for God's calling them out of slavery: that they might serve the one God and offer Him worship as the fulfillment of their humanity.

The zenith of Israel's ritual life commenced 480 years after their departure from Egypt, when Solomon began construction of the Temple, which presents, as it were, the coordination of all man's art and all man's skill in copying the work of God in Genesis. The gold that covers everything inside the Temple reflects the initial creation of light, a golden light that shines upon the forms of all created things, from gourds to cherubim to the great sea and the countless pomegranates and the endless variety of ornate fittings introduced by Hiram of Tyre. Fittingly, it takes Solomon seven years to complete his analog of the labor that the Lord accomplished in seven days.

Israel's ritual life was intimately tied to its national success, and, just as failures in worship led to the loss of the Ark to the Philistines, Israel's unfaithfulness led to the destruction of the Temple—and the disappearance of the Ark forever—during the invasion of the Babylonians. The Temple was at length rebuilt, though never, even with the improvements of Herod, did it reach its Solomonic grandeur again—and then that new temple was ultimately destroyed by the Romans in A.D. 70.

The stage had been set, though, for a new kind of worship, one tied to neither land nor altar nor temple but one that, through the incarnate body of God, elevated man to a place amid the eternal choirs who chant God's glory on high. "Destroy this temple," said Jesus, "and in three days I will raise it up" (John 2:19). When Jesus died, the veil of the Temple was torn, the barrier between Heaven and earth parting at last as the Church was born of the blood and water flowing from Christ's side. And this Church, this Body of Christ, formed through sacrificial sharing in the blood of the Lamb, no longer depended for its worship on walls of gold or arks. The Church, beginning with Mary, from whom Christ took His flesh, was the true Ark of the Covenant.

The immediate implication of the eucharistic character of the Church and her liturgical life is that she does not depend upon a building. She is constructed of her Groom and of the people, beginning with St. John and Mary, who make up His Body, His Bride. Christ became the new temple, torn down and raised again on the third day, made known to His disciples throughout time in the breaking of the bread.[138] Thus Minucius Felix wrote that "we have no temples; we have no altars."[139] The early Church, though

---

[138] See Luke 24:30-31. The lineaments of the Mass, with the breaking open of the Word in Scripture and the Word in the Bread of Life, may in some respects be discerned even more strongly after the Resurrection than at the Last Supper. Of course, neither the Last Supper nor the meal on the road took place within a ritually ordained space.

[139] Quoted in Peter G. Cobb, "The Architectural Setting of the Liturgy," in Cheslyn Jones et al., eds., *The Study of Liturgy*, rev. ed. (London: SPCK, 1992), 473-474.

her members often participated in the life of the synagogue, was centered on the home, whether in those of individual members of the Way or in homes set aside for the purpose. The catacombs supply some of the most eloquent examples of the kind of radiant homelessness which characterized the first generations of Christians.[140]

Following the Edict of Milan, Christianity became a highly visible aspect of public life through the construction of the first great basilicas. These seem to have exemplified that noble simplicity to which Trent and Vatican II direct our attention, with a long nave, illuminated by clerestory windows, directing the eyes of the Body to the sacrifice of the Head. Indeed, the early basilicas bear a notable resemblance to Noah's Ark, with its three-hundred-cubit length illuminated by the one-cubit opening that served as a window.

Few of the early basilicas have survived to our day, though our cultural imagination continues to be formed by the grand cathedrals of the Middle Ages, from Notre Dame in Paris to Chartres to Rouen, as well as the ornate feats of the Renaissance, like St. Peter's Basilica and Il Gesù in Rome. Taken together, the Church's architectural heritage presents one of the supreme treasures of Christendom.

Part of what these treasures remind us of, however, is the fact that the "Church has not adopted any particular style of art as her very own; she has admitted styles from every period according to the natural talents and circumstances of peoples, and the needs of the various rites."[141] The Eucharist, as a constant cosmic celebration, may in fact be celebrated anywhere, whether in St.

---

[140] See, for example, Matthew 8:20: "The Son of Man has nowhere to lay his head."

[141] *Sacrosanctum Concilium*, no. 123.

Peter's Basilica or on the "humble altar of a country church" or atop a stone beside the resounding sea.[142] Nonetheless, Vatican II commands, "When churches are to be built, let great care be taken that they be suitable for the celebration of liturgical services and for the active participation of the faithful."[143]

How, then, can architecture suit itself to the liturgy and draw the faithful into active participation therein, overcoming those very human tendencies of sensuality and mental distension whereby sloth leads us away from our proper end? Let us consider this in three phases: First, how can church architecture adequately direct our senses to their proper use; second, how can church architecture harmonize our sensual and spiritual faculties through encounters with the beautiful and the sublime; and third, how can architecture soothe our temporal and spatial anxiety by illuminating our harmonized faculties with the light of eternity?

Guiding the Senses

We have seen that our sense capacities contain in their very exercise the possibility of distraction and thus of capitulation to the power of sloth, which seeks to draw our attention away from God's will for us in the present moment as manifested by our given surroundings. Well-constructed churches of any artistic tradition take account of our propensity to distraction and restore our senses to their proper use, not by depriving us of them, but by directing them.

Consider, for example, the importance of the nave, the column, and light itself in properly disposing the attention of our senses during worship. The nave, by its length alone, draws the

---

[142] Pope John Paul II, Encyclical Letter on the Eucharist in Relation to the Church *Ecclesia de Eucharistia* (April 17, 2003), no. 8.

[143] *Sacrosanctum Concilium*, no. 124.

eye along itself to its end—the sanctuary—where the altar and the tabernacle comprise the locus of the liturgical action, making present on earth in our own time both what happened in Jerusalem two millennia ago and what is eternally occurring in the heavenly Jerusalem. Adornments to the nave and its side aisles, whether in the form of statuary, painting, or stained glass, should direct the eyes to the altar both by their form (so that the predominant lines of design lead the eye gently but inexorably toward the altar) and by their content (so that in looking at the stained glass face of a saint or at a marble Virgin, we are reminded of the one in whom the saints and Mary fixed all their hope and tender devotion). In a well-constructed church, as my gaze drifts to the left, the gesture of a stone angel or the eyes of a stained-glass St. Francis turn me back toward Christ. As I glance to the right, I see a painting of the crucified Lord, and I recall that dread day on Calvary and the glorious renewal of Sunday morning to which Mass makes me present anew.

The length of the nave should also remind us that, in Mass, we are being directed to our end, and so every effort should be made to celebrate Mass *ad orientem*, that is, facing East. Cardinal Ratzinger deplores the loss of *ad orientem* celebration as one of the crudest devolutions in liturgy after Vatican II. Even if it is the sad case that many churches are no longer constructed *ad orientem*, we may at least still take the step of orienting ourselves within the church to the crucifix and the tabernacle, which should always form the focal point to which the thrust of the nave directs us, the pilgrim People of God sailing toward eternity.[144]

Likewise, columns serve several critical purposes in stilling the eyes and guiding the attention. First, they add to the horizontal

---

[144] Ratzinger, *Spirit of the Liturgy*, 80–84.

thrust of the nave a vertical dimension of worship, their formal structure directing our gaze heavenward and reminding us that placing ourselves upon the altar with Christ is the means of our being lifted up with the Son of Man (see John 3:13–15 and 8:28). Second, the use of columns reminds man of his own stature and of his responsibility within the cosmos. As Roger Scruton notes, the column is the simplest possible artistic rendering of man himself, standing upright among the rest of the animals. Just as the weight of a church rests heavily on its columns, so the weight of the cosmos lies upon man, both in his capacity to cultivate and uphold the beauty of creation and so give glory to the Creator and in his sharing in the life of the Creator through Christ's Incarnation and Paschal Mystery. Third, the column marks off a sacred space. The portico of a church, with its line of columns across the front, calls man to enter while reminding him that, within these precincts, he will find himself drawn beyond the ordinary concerns of the world, beyond the mundane limitations of time and space, into an endless place that is touched with eternity.

In the liturgy, we bask in the light of the eighth day, in the re-creation of the visible light of the first day by the Resurrection of the Word, who is Himself the uncreated light we recall in the Creed. The disposition of the physical light whereby we see in turn forms our perception of that spiritual light whereby all things are illumined by God's grace. Natural light plays a critical role in worship, with the heavenly light of clerestory windows illuminating our worship without distracting us with visions of the outer world. The transformation of light by stained glass also reminds us of the re-creation taking place in the heavenly liturgy. Ground-level windows facing directly into the street, on the other hand, windows which admit light and with it the vision of all the regular goings-on in the world, can be deeply detrimental to properly disposing the senses.

To all this it should be added that we ourselves, as the real, enduring architecture of the Church, should above all else serve to guide our neighbors' attention to Christ. Looking about during Mass, we should be guided back to the crucifix, the tabernacle, and the altar by the living gazes of our fellow worshippers. There is nothing that directs our gaze so profoundly as the gaze of another.

Now that we understand how good architecture and ornamentation gently guide our senses to their proper use, let us turn to examine how they harmonize our sense powers with our higher capacities of imagination and intellect, specifically through the aesthetic experiences of the beautiful and the sublime.

Beauty and the Sublime

All churches should be beautiful. St. Thomas Aquinas says that the beautiful is that which, having been seen, pleases.[145] This is a simple definition, so simple as at first to seem inadequate to proper aesthetics. Yet in its simplicity it both allows for the broadest possible range of aesthetic experience and incorporates the several human faculties needed for comprehension of beauty. We say, for example, that a sunset is beautiful on account of the feeling of simple pleasure that attends the sensory input of the westering sun striking the infinitely various clouds and touching off waves of gold and salmon color. We call Botticelli's *The Birth of Venus* beautiful for its soft suffusion of color and the loveliness of Venus herself, emerging from the spray of the sea. We call Mozart's

[145] St. Thomas Aquinas, *Summa Theologica* I, q. 5, art. 4, reply to objection 1.

Clarinet Concerto beautiful as the sweet notes of the clarinet drift gently over us, soothing our spirits.

But there are other kinds of beauty, and we call many things beautiful which are not pleasing in the simple way of the examples above. We call Mozart's *Requiem* beautiful, as well as Grünewald's Isenheim altar *Crucifixion*. Neither is so sweetly uplifting as a Monet or a sunrise. And that is because their beauty does not operate in the mere satisfaction of sense appetites but rather in the harmonization of the sense faculties with the intellect. The mind, recognizing the grave intensity of death, finds in Mozart's *Requiem* a sense experience suited to that moment of harsh expectancy. Grünewald's *Crucifixion*, demonstrating the true physical horror of the moment in every detail, from the lacerations on Jesus' body to the cruelly contorted finger of St. John the Baptist to the abiding darkness behind the Lord, accords with our intellectual recognition of the ultimate terror of a moment in which God Himself feels abandoned by God. And so the image, not sensually pleasing, nonetheless causes pleasure in the harmonization of sense and intellect in the imagination.

Church architecture makes use of such an aesthetic by harmonizing our senses with our imagination and intellect, primarily through the power of symbols. Consider the north rose window in the Cathedral of Notre Dame. Its images of saints and angels not only give imaginative content for the orientation of our minds toward the things of Heaven, but they also, by their arrangement, draw us into the eighth-day light of the Resurrection. The central image of Mary and the infant Christ, with Mary as the crown of creation and the son she bore as the Creator, is surrounded by eight decorative roundels, the number eight reminding us that the work of creation is ultimately directed beyond the passage of the temporal world to the enduring heavenly world into which all the goodness of creation has been called. The eight are then multiplied to sixteen panels as our eye moves outward from the central image; the sixteen then themselves doubling to two outer courses of thirty-two scenes. Our minds, internalizing such images, are formed for a kind of thinking that steps beyond the concerns of daily life in order to taste the things of eternity, which in turn allows us to focus more properly on life's daily labors, transmuting the light of the world into the heavenly light of the stained glass, which illuminates the minds of worshippers.

When our minds begin to operate on this symbolic level—when we begin to recognize the significance of the priest ascending the steps to the sanctuary, or of the wax of the Paschal candle dripping into the baptismal font on Holy Saturday, or of a server in the Latin Mass holding the end of the priest's chasuble so that we, the people, like the woman with a hemorrhage, can touch the hem of Christ's garment—we become ever more deeply aware of the manner in which presence at the Mass is presence at the heavenly liturgy, which in turn pervades our awareness of every moment of life.

The beautiful harmonization of our senses and our intellect through the symbolic imagination thus educates us in worship. Alongside the beautiful, experience of the sublime also operates to elevate our attention and emphasize the awful grandeur of God's love for us. The sublime, argues Kant, consists of an experience of something so vast and mighty as to completely overwhelm our human sense capacities, an experience which nonetheless leads to further awe at the fact that our intellects themselves can expand to meet the vastness of the object before us. When we encounter a whale, for instance, or see the night sky in its unadulterated glory, we meet something which is, on a physical level, far superior to ourselves. Yet the power of the human mind, acknowledging that greatness, itself expands to the limit of that greatness and reasserts man's significance before the overwhelming object.[146] Hence King Lear, encountering the storm into which the cruelty of his daughters has thrust him, learns his humanity again and takes pity on the fool who accompanies him.[147]

The intensity of sublime experience reaches an even keener pitch when man is confronted with God. The great theophanies of the Old Testament, from God's answer to Job to Moses' meeting with the Lord on the mountain, attest to the fact that mere man cannot, however great his mind, measure up to the infinite power and majesty of God. The only response he can give in the end, far from understanding the mystery he encounters, is to fall down in worship, to praise the Lord who gives all things, and to admit, "I have spoken but did not understand; things too marvelous for me, which I did not know. . . . Therefore I disown what I have said, and repent in dust and ashes" (Job 42:3, 6).

The vast cathedrals of Christendom may in themselves provide an experience of the sublime. Entering St. Peter's Basilica, for example, or Santa Maria Maggiore, or the basilica at Assisi, who has not felt himself stilled by the vastness of the space and the grandeur of the design and the labor needed to erect it?

Physical vastness is often key to the experience of the sublime, and so not all liturgical spaces can be sublime in themselves. A humble country church or even a small urban parish, however beautiful—Santa Maria della Vittoria in Rome, for example, where Bernini's *St. Teresa in Ecstasy* is housed—simply lacks the stature to be physically sublime. However, part of the specific character

---

[146] See Robert E. Wood, *Placing Aesthetics: Reflections on the Philosophic Tradition* (Athens: Ohio University Press, 1999), 137.
[147] See Shakespeare, *King Lear*, 3.2.

of liturgical space is that it draws us beyond the physical to the spiritual—faith, as Hebrews puts it, allows us to see that the "visible came into being through the invisible" (Heb. 11:3). What is more, this invisible reality, unlike the grandest of visible realities, cannot be fathomed by our minds, even when they exert their greatest efforts. Thus, even in the smallest church, even at a Mass sacrificed on the shore of the sea or on a mountain slope or in a prison cell, we may be liturgically drawn into the presence of the Almighty before whom our capacities fail, in an experience which supersedes the grandest limits of the earthly sublime.

What is more astonishing still is that this sacred rite, this sacrificial offering of the Son, makes us partakers in that sublime love which so overwhelms mere man. For, through God's Incarnation and Resurrection, through being made one with the head, we, the Body of Christ, are given a share in the divine life. And to ponder this mystery is always to enter into greater depths of wonder.

All churches, then, should be beautiful—that is, the art and architecture should set our senses in a harmonious relationship with our intellect through inviting us into the imaginative depths of the liturgy. And this beauty, even in the simplest space, should open the way for an experience of the sublime mysteries to which God has called us from eternity.

Against Anxiety

Good architecture directs our senses to their richest possible use, turning us away from acedia's skewed vision of reality so that we might begin to see as God sees and to rejoice with God in the goodness of creation. Likewise, it harmonizes our senses with our intellects through the imaginative experience of the beautiful and sublime, experience which further rejects the complaints of acedia and calls us to love the end to which God has ordered us. Finally, this harmonization soothes the anxiety occasioned by our experience of time, giving us a share of that eternal perspective whereby we become capable of viewing the other through the eyes of Christ.

With our faculties properly ordered to each other and so to their contemplative end, we become ever more proof against the vicissitudes of time. Attention to the things of eternity grants us respite from the temporal distension which, according to St. Augustine, occasions so much of our anxiety. Likewise, it trains us to avoid the spatial distension, the constant tendency of our minds, exacerbated by technology, to leap away from our concrete circumstances into fantasy realms where we imagine we might at last be fulfilled. Good architecture, directing our attention not to the outside world or to our neighbor, draws us, with our neighbor and the rest of the world, onto the altar of the Cross.

The more accustomed we grow to living in the contemplative mode that is our end, the more our usual temporal anxiety can be transformed into the anxiety of Christ, the anxiety of being drawn out on the Cross. This is far from the anxiety of sin to which we usually fall prey and which is a key factor in sloth's depredations. It is the anxiety of kenosis, of going to the very limit of things, of going to the ragged edge of being, the unfinished hem of the cloak, to extend the saving power of God to the fallen, the broken, the bleeding.

Our churches should thus express the reality of our worship, which is not simply a communal meal but a sacrifice of man to God in God, who Himself makes the meal efficacious, uniting men and women to that sacrifice so that they can be justified with the justification Christ alone can offer.

In this way, the liturgy, showing us what it means to live in the House of God, demonstrates to us that all the world is a theater of worship. Attuned to the aesthetics of the divine, all places and times become for us occasions for rejoicing in the goodness of creation and the affirmative gaze of the Creator. We become like the singer of Psalm 84, who cries, "How lovely your dwelling, O LORD of hosts!... As the sparrow finds a home and the swallow a nest to settle her young, My home is by your altars, LORD of hosts, my king and my God!" (Ps. 84:2, 4). Our home, the place where we should settle our young, is the heavenly Jerusalem, and well-built churches show us that the heavenly Jerusalem is itself the foundation of the earth. Those who dwell in God's house, those whose consciousness is trained to recognize the marks of the Lord in every place, praise God at all times, leaving aside the anxieties of time for the joy of eternity. The man who enthrones his heart with Christ on the altar of the Cross will "go from strength to strength" (Ps. 84:7, KJV). Good architecture, strengthening our sight, refining our imagination, allows us to see that this earth is itself the house of God.

Having considered how architecture can transform space so as to elevate our experience of the liturgy, we now examine how sacred music can similarly transform time, teaching us to live, like Christ, in the presence of the Father who is eternally present to us.

6

Sacred Time: The Music of the Liturgy

Some scholars maintain that one of the oldest compositions in all of Scripture is Exodus 15, which begins: "I will sing to the LORD, for he is gloriously triumphant; horse and chariot he has cast into the sea."[148] The first recorded note of Scripture is thus a revelry of praise to the Lord who had redeemed His people, bringing them out of Egypt through the stilled chaos of the sea. And the last note of Scripture, the revelation of the heavenly liturgy, takes its key from this same song: "On the sea of glass were standing those who had won the victory over the beast and its image and the number that signified its name. They were holding God's harps, and they sang the song of Moses" (Rev. 15:2–3). The whole history of salvation revolves around the joy of the People of God who have been led out from the rule of Pharaoh, from the rule of Satan, into the glory of redemption, a joy and a glory that break forth in song.

Indeed, song is woven throughout Scripture in sweet testament to the fact that, as St. Augustine, put it, "Only the lover sings."[149]

---

[148] See note for Exodus 15:1–21, United States Conference of Catholic Bishops, https://bible.usccb.org/bible/exodus/15.

[149] St. Augustine, Sermon 336.

From the laments of Job to the psalms to the Magnificat, Scripture lets forth strains of the most tender poetry, expressing God's love for His people and the people's broken-hearted turning away from and back toward Him.

Music, moreover, attends the theophanic moments that reveal the true worship toward which God calls His people. At Sinai, we hear the blasts of the trumpets. And, in Revelation, we witness the songs of the angelic choirs: *Sanctus, sanctus, sanctus*. We join in this song in the liturgy, allowing our meager words to be taken up into the Word's exultant praise in the supper of the Lamb.

We remain with Israel between the Red Sea and the end of time, where our participation in the liturgy Christ established for the chosen race, thereby fulfilling the promise to Abraham, continues as a pilgrim participation, a contemplative taste, a snatch of the divine music. What, then, do we do? As Hopkins said, "Praise him."[150] The Church Militant, like the Israelites of old, must march with Judah, whose name means praise, at her head. And what is it to praise but to sing?

> Rejoice, you righteous, in the LORD;
>> praise from the upright is fitting.
> Give thanks to the LORD on the harp;
>> on the ten-stringed lyre offer praise.
> Sing to him a new song;
>> skillfully play with joyful chant. (Ps. 33:1–3)

We render praise in singing that liturgy whereby Christ taught us how to worship, bringing to fruition the education begun at Sinai.

---

[150] Gerard Manley Hopkins, "Pied Beauty," available at Poem Analysis, https://poemanalysis.com/gerard-manley-hopkins/pied-beauty/.

Music, then, forms the liturgical fabric of the life of Israel, giving forth resplendent witness to God's glory at the end of the first step in Israel's long road of learning to worship properly, and then again resounding through all ages into eternity. It is for this liturgical character that *Sacrosanctum Concilium* praises sacred music in the highest terms: "The musical tradition of the universal Church is a treasure of inestimable value, greater even than that of any other art. The main reason for this pre-eminence is that, as sacred song united to the words, it forms a necessary or integral part of the solemn liturgy."[151]

Much as in the case of architecture, though, we of the latter-day Church frequently find our ears confronted with an impoverished attempt at music. Our choirs, singing along to a guitarist who is strumming the chords of pop music beside the altar, elicit not so much awe as pity, or perhaps even a species of saccharine malaise. Often enough, the pieces composed over the past fifty years employ such trite abstractions as to fail to capture our imagination at all; at other times, their rhymes, as in Dan Schutte's "Glory and Praise to Our God," play so fast and loose with the language as to flirt with heresy: "Though the power of sin prevails, / Our God is here to save." No doubt our God is here to save, but to speak of sin's prevailing is to come dangerously close to denying Christ's promise that the gates of Hell should not prevail against His Church.

For all the paucity of good music, of real music, in our ecclesial life, song nonetheless remains one of the surest means of raising the mind and heart to God, of attuning our senses to the perception of invisible realities and thus harmonizing our faculties for the performance of God's will. In considering the importance of music, we shall first examine how music, as the artistic rendering

[151] *Sacrosanctum Concilium*, no. 112.

of time itself, teaches us to attend to eternity and so overcomes the temporal ravages of sloth which so threaten Sunday observance. We shall then consider the cultural influences that have eaten so cancerously at our musical tradition. Finally, we will observe certain characteristics of good music, with *Sacrosanctum Concilium*, *Tra le Sollecitudini*, and Scripture as our guides.

The Art of Time

All human experience of art depends upon our awareness of time, and thus upon our faculties of memory and anticipation. Though we may intuit the whole of a church or of a painting, we nonetheless attend to the specific details of these, and especially of sculpture, through time, only arriving at a full appreciation of a work by long study and contemplation from every angle. The unification of temporal experience as a whole is most dramatically demonstrated in music.

Music, says Hegel, is the most spiritual of art forms, the one that, because it is the least material, has the capacity to penetrate the soul most deeply.[152] This power is dependent upon our ability to remember and to look forward. To listen to music without memory and anticipation would be to hear a string of sounds without real or logical connection. The effect would undoubtedly be jarring in the extreme, as a single note of music encountered at random is indeed heard to be. Rather, when we hear a piece of music, we experience in brief some of the emotional variance of tension and resolution that forms the fabric of our earthly lives. We learn to recall pleasing motifs and to detect in even the most inharmonious passages the possibility of a future fulfillment. In short, music is the master class in the school of time. It trains us

---

[152] See Wood, *Placing Aesthetics*, 179.

not simply to live in the moment, but rather to allow moments to be woven together through art and so elevated to the eternal. Good music thus becomes inimical to sloth, which wants to use time to draw our minds out of God's presence. Good music, whether sacred, devotional, or secular, teaches us the patience that is the pathway to eternity.

We all have experienced the temporal power of music: it relaxes us, it enthuses us, and, more than any other sense experiences except for smell, it "takes us back," as we say. We use music, whether we consider it in such terms or not, to shape our experience of time's passage, and indeed, in many cases, to escape from the feeling of that passage. In the best music, it is not simply that we escape from the order of the workaday world, but rather we are handed back the world in its beauty and reminded of the end to which all beauty calls us. On the other hand, music can, by suiting itself to our passions, incite us to the service of those passions. Much modern pop music, for instance, dwells at such grotesque length on the prosecution of lust, the pursuit of money, and the desire for revenge upon our enemies, that we can hardly hear the words and their throbbing, driving settings without being drawn into sympathy with them. The children of Israel, having just joined in the Song of Miriam, shortly thereafter join in the songs of abandon at the foot of Sinai as they worship the golden calf. Joshua, coming down from the mountain, believes that he hears the sounds of battle, but Moses corrects him: what they hear is the sound of singing (see Exod. 32).

Music thus has the capacity either to gather up our temporal experience and cast it in the light of eternity or to seek to snatch a false emotional satisfaction from the passage of time. We turn now to consider the ways contemporary popular music has tended in the latter direction, with the results spilling over into the music of the liturgy.

False Music

Music, as Plato knew well, trains the soul, establishing those harmonies which resonate within the person through life.[153] And, Shakespeare warns, "The man that hath no music in himself, / Nor is not moved with concord of sweet sounds, / Is fit for treasons, stratagems, and spoils; / The motions of his spirit are dull as night, / And his affections dark as Erebus. / Let no such man be trusted. Mark the music."[154] Our call is to join the heavenly chorus which sings eternal praise to the Father, Son, and Holy Spirit.

Painting, sculpture, and poetry—the fine arts generally—have tended to be placed on the periphery of modern life, seen as ornaments, indulgences, and hobbies, little connected with the real business of living.[155] Music, however, enjoys unwavering devotion. Our offices are filled with music during working hours. We listen to songs in elevators, in waiting rooms, and in our cars. Earbuds keep us plugged in as we jog or check our e-mail or walk from the subway to the workspace.

While the experience of authentic beauty always provides an encounter with God, failed attempts to produce the beautiful may in themselves prove a profound hindrance to such an encounter. Just as we expect priests—indeed all Christians—to be holy, to be a people set apart and striving always for deeper holiness, and as any wickedness on the part of the Christian and especially on the part of the priest may serve to drive the unbelieving further into unbelief, so too can music that fails to be beautiful or that otherwise falls short of its liturgical purpose be an affront to believer and nonbeliever alike. That which sets itself nearest to God should, we

[153] Plato, *Republic*, bk. 4.
[154] Shakespeare, *The Merchant of Venice*, 5.1.
[155] Walker Percy, "Physician as Novelist," in *Message in the Bottle*, 192.

reason, partake most clearly of the divine splendor; anything which does not do so, or is not at least seen to strive for such excellence to the utmost of its capacities, may be a source of scandal.

Such, unfortunately, is the case with much of our contemporary liturgical music. While perhaps far from training us in the way of sin (as much pop music does) or from teaching heresy, a great many of the songs that are sung in our Catholic churches on Sundays are simply poor compositions. They do not pass the test of art, and so they cannot pass the test of Christianity. Then, too, these mediocre songs often take a special mediocrity from the quality of our musicians. Great music calls for great talent and long practice, and the pitiable fact is that many church choirs, though perhaps devout and deeply earnest, lack the skill to perform such music as will unify worshippers' perception of time in the exaltation of praise that elevates consciousness to eternity. And, indeed, it bears remembering that sacred music is not meant for performance but rather for prayer.

Indeed, we might well group all the faults of contemporary liturgical music under the heading of distraction. Too often, our music draws us away from the proper object of worship. Too often, it subjects us to the anxiety-ridden mental distension by which Augustine characterizes time. Too often, it cooperates with sloth in leading us to despise that worship which is our proper end and the passage to eternity. This has happened in many ways. Here we take up three of these ways which may be connected with the influence of popular music: the secular liturgy of music and its celebration of the performer, the usage of the guitar and the piano, and the dependence on banal and simplistic musical patterns which make little demand on the soul of the listener and suggest easy resolutions.[156]

---

[156] It is worth noting here that predictability in music is not of itself detrimental to liturgical use. In fact, such predictability can be

The Voodoo Music and Arts Experience, a three-day festival traditionally held over Halloween weekend in New Orleans, featured a simple slogan for many years: "Worship the music." While few Americans would express their listening habits in such idolatrous terms, once again the way we dispose of our time tends to give away our underlying devotions. Most Americans listen to between three and four hours of music daily—that is, roughly one Lord's Day's worth of each week is spent listening to music.[157] Whether we say so or not, we do worship music.

We should take some measure of comfort in the thought that popular devotion to music, the most spiritual of art forms, hints at the public yearning to hear that music which eternally attends the heavenly throne. We should remember, too, that those monks who chant the Divine Office spend immense quantities of time immersed in music; even listening to it can be a means of preparing for the chorus of God's court.

But the vast majority of the music that fuels our commutes, thumps through our shopping trips, and spurs our late-night study sessions aims not at the glory of God but at the fame and enrichment of the performer and the glamorization of lust and greed. The entertainers themselves often become sexual idols and models of consumptive excess, and many of us, watching them on television or listening over the radio, fantasize about living as they do and drawing the adoration of the crowds.

---

useful to the singers and congregation who are praying the words of that music. But the predictability of a hymn ought to be of a different character from that of a pop song.

[157] Marie Charlotte Götting, "Weekly Time Spent with Music, 2015–2019," Statista, December 8, 2021, https://www.statista.com/statistics/828195/time-spent-music/.

In many cases, the relationship of pop star to audience has come to serve as paradigm for that between liturgical musician and the worshippers. Placed on or just beside the altar, even the most decorous and talented musicians prove deeply distracting, drawing the attention of worshippers away from the sacrifice of the Mass. This need not be so. In the early centuries of the church, it was common for choirs to be arrayed about the altar in imitation of the angelic choirs arrayed around the throne of God.[158] But the angelic choirs seek not to perform for those of us watching but rather, by praising God, they draw us into the song of praise. In short, the singers of liturgical music should themselves be subservient to the song, which lifts the minds and hearts of those present to God, a consideration which led Pope St. Pius X to suggest that singers, humbly vested, should be concealed behind a grille so as not to distract the congregation.[159] Many modern church choirs, on the other hand, comport themselves like those giving a performance, looking to the crowd for affirmation. But the liturgy is not a performance. It is a prayer.

Any organization, Aristotle says, constitutes a genus. A family unites each of its members. A corporation makes all of its members parts of its body. All of being is itself a genus proceeding from God and directed toward Him. A work of art has a way of establishing a genus among the artist, the work, and the observer. The liturgy, as the supreme work of divine art, is established for the sake of unifying, to call into the genus of covenant God and His people. The danger of art within the church, especially within the context of the Mass, is that it may draw the observer into a subsidiary genus with the work and the human artist. While poor musicians can

[158] Cobb, "Architectural Setting," 475.
[159] Pope Pius X, *Tra Le Sollecitudini*, no. 14.

be distracting, it is in fact thus the greatest musicians who pose the greatest threat to true worship.

I recall, for example, a very large Mass held for all teachers of the Archdiocese of New Orleans. The gathered assembly was too large for any church, so we celebrated Mass in a convention center. All in all, the liturgy was well celebrated, but the handling of music proved especially distracting. The musicians, comprising two groups—one who sang in English, the other in Spanish—took turns at the left of the stage erected to serve as sanctuary. Their position was thus quite prominent. But, as though this were not enough, on either side of the sanctuary were two large screens on which the video of the Mass was relayed, presumably for the benefit of those seated far off. No such screens are employed in the regular conventions and graduations held at this center. Perhaps we can make allowance for a desire that those present at Mass be more present than those at any old convention.

In any case, the nadir of the affair fell when, during the lengthy distribution of Communion, the cameras remained fixed on the musicians, who could easily have played at the jazz and blues clubs of Frenchman Street, so skilled were they, to the point of redeeming several of the most humdrum modern hymns, making them feel like real songs. Yet, as the distribution progressed, the attention of the crowd, which for a long time drifted into desultory and very audible conversation, shifted more and more to the musicians. The fundamental relationship established was not between God and His people but between the musicians and their audience. How much more good those cameras could have done had they been pointed at the altar and the crucifix!

This affirmation is most easily gained through the use of those methods which have won our pop stars great fame. For instance, the guitar and the piano have served as the instrumental bases for most of the last century's pop sensations. Most of us are accustomed to hearing these two instruments in our parishes. Pope St. Pius X, however, explicitly condemned the piano for liturgical use, along with all other noisy and frivolous instruments, in *Tra Le Sollecitudini*.[160] While we might contest his classifications on the grounds that the piano, and, dare we say, the drum and the guitar, can be put to lofty use, we can little deny that they are not so used in our churches today. This is so because our liturgical compositions for guitar and piano follow the same musical structures of pop songs, with sequences of chords playing out all too predictably.[161]

That is, while sacred music ought to lead us to participate in the sacrifice of the Mass and so draw closer to God, much of the music we hear during Mass today leads us to participate in the musicians' performance and thus to collapse our attention upon the singers and upon ourselves.[162]

---

[160] Ibid., no. 19.

[161] We should remember, too, that beauty can be measured not only by the thing in itself but by its proportionality to its setting. This means that, though the music of Rush or Yes is often quite lovely, emotionally stirring, and technically proficient — far beyond the measure of the songs of Dan Schutte or Marty Haugen — because their works are unsuited to a liturgical context, they would become ugly if employed there.

[162] I recall a pilgrimage to Heart's Home in upstate New York several years ago. A former opera singer performed several pieces as pilgrims gathered in prayer near an outdoor structure housing a statue of the crucified Lord. Among the other pieces, she sang a few hymns, which garnered only the most desultory participation from those gathered. When she sang "Let It Be," though, nearly all joined with her in full-throated chorus. It is worth asking why the Beatles inspire such devotion, but our modern hymnodists do not. McCartney's formal characteristics are very often copied by the latter artists, yet it is the Beatles who have set forth a liturgy

Real Music

So much, then, for beauty's counterfeit. What sort of music should we hear at Mass? What forms of song are suited to the liturgy, fit to shake off the specter of sloth and compel us to rejoice in the beauty of our divine call?

In Scripture

Scripture itself gives us no small measure of guidance in the matter. The Songs of Miriam and Moses, bookmarking the actual composition of Scripture, invite us to lift our voices in praise. The psalms supply a superb catalogue of the themes which should make up liturgical song. The Song of Daniel and Mary's Magnificat recall the goodness of creation and the manner in which the soul of man multiplies that goodness. Likewise, the Bible lists many of the instruments used in the liturgical moments of the life of Israel, from the blast of the ram's horn at Sinai to the sounding of the trumpets at the end of time. And the psalms often specify the instruments meant to accompany them, such as the timbrel and the harp.

The ram's horn and the timbrel may be little available for our use today, yet the texts of the psalms and of the rest of Scripture remain to guide our liturgical lyrics, which, intended to draw us into the life of the Word, can do no better than to use the words He has inspired. Moreover, if Scripture does not provide perfect prescriptions for our musical usage, it nonetheless supplies a fundamental attitude toward the Lord to be gathered up in music. We, God's people, are a people set apart, and our music must be holy, too.

---

that apparently captures the imagination of modern man more thoroughly.

Sacred Time: The Music of the Liturgy

Gregorian Chant, Sacred Polyphony, Hymnody – and Beyond

The Fathers of the Second Vatican Council, following Pope St. Pius X and Trent, note that Gregorian chant, as the form of music best suited to the Roman liturgy, should be given pride of place therein.[163] Simple, austere, and communal, chant embodies that poetry of word and elegance of melody which forever finds the freshness of language and freedom of sound most fitting for worship. It eschews the predictable sentiments and resolutions which make pop music such a ready salve for our workaday spirits and instead trains the heart to recognize the animated phrasing of the divine song. It is "the supreme model of all sacred music," "inherited from the ancient fathers."[164] It has, as it were, grown up alongside the Roman liturgy, and its restoration tends to restore the People of God.

While chant sounds foreign to many of us in this day and age, perhaps especially in a liturgical setting, it bears noting that the Gregorian model of music has served as the zenith of the art not only for the Church but also for the greatest classical masters. Mendelssohn and Mozart both expressed the highest admiration for chant, with Mozart going so far as to say that he would gladly trade all his musical output to have crafted a Gregorian prelude. And in fact many of the masters' Mass settings are themselves unsuitable for liturgical use, given their duration and complication.[165]

With chant, the Church celebrates polyphonic sacred music as highly suitable to the liturgy. As *Sacrosanctum Concilium* has

---

[163] *Sacrosanctum Concilium*, no. 116.

[164] Pope Pius X, *Tra Le Sollecitudini*, nos. 4, 3.

[165] Gerhard Gietmann, "Ecclesiastical Music," in *Catholic Encyclopedia*, vol. 10 (New York: Appleton, 1911), https://www.newadvent.org/cathen/10648a.htm.

it, "Other kinds of sacred music, especially polyphony, are by no means excluded from liturgical celebrations, so long as they accord with the spirit of the liturgical action."[166] St. Pius X places the high-water mark of polyphony at Palestrina in the sixteenth century.[167] The legend, indeed, is that Palestrina's *Missa Papae Marcelli* saved polyphony from Trent's chopping block by demonstrating authoritatively that polyphonic composition could be rendered in such a way as to remain intelligible to the worshipping assembly.

Alongside these ancient forms, the Church always permits and celebrates those modern modes of music that give glory to God and attune the heart to His worship. Pope St. Pius X confirms that the "Church has always recognized and favored the progress of the arts, admitting to the service of religion everything good and beautiful discovered by genius in the course of ages."[168] Nonetheless, this progress must always be harmonized with the liturgical laws, and so, while modern music produces works of the greatest "excellence, sobriety and gravity," its development from a stream of artistry dedicated chiefly to secular use demands that we use it only with the greatest caution.[169] Israel had to go out into the desert, not only with all her men and women and even her cattle but also with the spoils of the Egyptians. The form of their worship was not something to be determined of their own volition but rather waited upon the commands of God, who would indeed make use of that plundered silver and gold in the fashioning of the tabernacle and its implements. But that same gold was put to evil use by the Israelites when, waiting at

---

[166] *Sacrosanctum Concilium*, no. 116.
[167] *Tra Le Sollecitudini*, no. 4.
[168] Ibid., no. 5.
[169] Ibid.

the foot of Sinai, they took worship into their own hands and forged the golden calf.

Our own use of modern music in the liturgy often runs dangerously close to such idolatrous revelry, and it will not do for us, like Aaron, to fashion such forgeries and then to say that the cow simply came out of the fire and we don't know how. So many of our hymns, focusing on the congregation, employing the instruments of the pop stars and so formally echoing the themes of our modern debauch, and turning the Mass into a concert, draw our attention away from Christ and lead us to desire not so much to place ourselves on the altar with Him as to lavish praise on those performing beside Him. Nowhere is this more hideously felt than when a congregation, having chatted and dozed and checked its texts through Mass, suddenly applauds the musicians.

Then, too, those attempts at hymnody which ignore the criteria of sacred music, with much of the rest of our liturgical life, are often just so much more noise. They do not proceed from the great silence of prayer, nor do they flow into that great silence, and so "Mass becomes racket and confusion," as Thomas Merton put it.[170] Nonetheless, with chant and polyphony, hymns have formed a grand part of the Church's musical patrimony. The hymnal form itself stretches deep into the history of Israel, as in the Song of Miriam and especially in the psalms, which have enjoyed fervent devotion throughout the Church's history. Many passages in Paul's letters, too, especially Philippians 2:6-11, have been identified as early Christian hymns.[171]

---

[170] Thomas Merton, *The Sign of Jonas*, quoted in Robert Cardinal Sarah, with Nicolas Diat, *The Power of Silence: Against the Dictatorship of Noise*, trans. Michael J. Miller (San Francisco: Ignatius Press, 2017), 31.

[171] Esolen, *Real Music*, 27-28.

In his book *Real Music*, Anthony Esolen offers a compelling poetic study of hymns, demonstrating the profound impoverishment our music has undergone since Vatican II. While this musical degradation has mirrored the decline in sacred art and architecture, the loss of rich music is especially to be deplored insofar as music forms a more integral part of the liturgy than architecture. Today's hymnals, Esolen shows, are organized and edited with more concern for celebrating the community as it is than with praising and engaging the God who, by His death and Resurrection, forms that community—despite the people's recalcitrance. This hymnal whitewashing tends not only to expunge from the original texts masculine pronouns and frank admissions of man's guilt but also to adopt freely the forms of music popular in the secular realm. Thus we hear of "people" rather than "man," and we hear nothing of God as warrior or of mankind's evil. The result is that our modern hymns often strike the ear as uninspired imitations of the Beatles. They give the impression that, since sacred music is no different in kind from its popular counterpart, secular music may itself be employed in liturgical instances. Esolen cites the horrid use of Sinatra's "My Way" in funeral Masses and offers the very sound rule of thumb that any song Satan could proudly sing will certainly not do for liturgical uses.[172]

On the other hand, sound liturgical music, by form as well as content, lifts the heart and mind to God, inviting each of us to see ourselves as we are and so to turn more authentically to the God who has saved us. Taking *Sacrosanctum Concilium* and the consequent text, *Musicam Sacram*, as guides, we now look briefly at some principles to be observed in fostering good music.

[172] Ibid., 12–13, 250.

Sacred Time: The Music of the Liturgy

Aims, Characteristics, and Principles of Sacred Music

All arts take their operations from their ends. Sacred music has two aims: "the glory of God and the sanctification of the faithful."[173] Therefore, the use and composition of music and the liturgy should be ruled by these two goals. It should thus have "a certain holy sincerity of form" and should draw the faithful into active participation.[174]

As to the formal characteristics of sacred music, the Church does not only pass down a great treasury of works, including "Gregorian chant, sacred polyphony in its various forms ... sacred music for the organ ... and sacred popular music."[175] She also encourages the composition of new works which "grow organically from forms already existing."[176] She urges composers to "cultivate sacred music and increase its store of treasures" in order to provide "for the active participation of the entire assembly of the faithful."[177]

It is perhaps the notion of "active participation" which causes the greatest difficulty in successfully executing sacred music in our parishes. For while one "cannot find anything more religious and more joyful in sacred celebrations than a whole congregation expressing its faith and devotion in song," nonetheless, active participation is "above all internal, in the sense that by it the faithful join their mind to what they pronounce or hear, and cooperate with heavenly grace."[178] The outward elements of observance, such

---

[173] *Sacrosanctum Concilium*, no. 112.

[174] Vatican Council II, Instruction on Music in the Liturgy *Musicam Sacram* (March 5, 1967), no. 4a.

[175] Ibid., no. 4b.

[176] *Sacrosanctum Concilium*, no. 23.

[177] Ibid., no. 121.

[178] *Musicam Sacram*, nos. 16, 15a.

as singing, then become embodied signs of the inward life tending toward its heavenly fulfillment.

With this in mind, the Church teaches that generally "worship is given a more noble form when it is celebrated in song."[179] And when circumstances limit the degree to which song can be incorporated into the celebration of the Mass, priority should be given to those parts of the Mass that "are by their nature of greater importance, and especially those which are to be sung by the priest ... with the people replying, or those which are to be sung by the priest and people together."[180] *Musicam Sacram* delineates the liturgical celebration according to three degrees based on their importance to the liturgy, with the hope that the faithful will be led into ever richer participation therein.

The first degree includes the priestly greeting and the people's reply, the Gospel acclamation, "the prayer over the offerings; the preface with its dialogue and the Sanctus; the final doxology of the Canon, the Lord's prayer with its introduction and embolism; the Pax Domini; the prayer after the Communion; the formulas of dismissal."[181] The second degree incorporates the Kyrie, Gloria, Agnus Dei, Creed, and Prayer of the Faithful. And the third involves processional songs, the Offertory hymn, and the readings of Sacred Scripture. This order of priority can perhaps shed some light on the ways our use of music in the liturgy has gone wrong and how it can be reinvigorated. For in many parishes emphasis seems rather to be given to the processionals and the Offertory, with a premium often being placed on using such songs as will draw the greatest participation from the congregation. Oftentimes

---

[179] Ibid., no. 5.
[180] Ibid., no. 7.
[181] Ibid., no. 29c.

the works chosen are for this reason more properly devotional than liturgical.

Composer and conductor Paul Jernberg indicates seven principles we might follow in the renewal of sacred music. Each of these can help us to reframe our understanding of liturgical music and how we can foster the glory of God and the active participation of the faithful for their sanctification.

The first is that music clothes the text of the Mass.[182] It is not mere addition or ornamentation, but rather it gives deeper embodiment to the spiritual reality of the Lamb's Supper. On this point we can also emphasize the importance of ensuring that liturgical music, as clothing to a scriptural action, should be scriptural in nature. The Mass, as the sacrament of the Word, should be for us a school of Scripture, forming our imaginations to the contours of the Bible. Liturgical music should thus draw much of its text from Scripture itself and, when it does not use the Bible's words, should at least reflect on those words in humble meditation.[183]

The second is that this music is primarily vocal. As such, it engages the human mind, soul, and body in an intimate way. We have noted before the importance of language to human life. It is through our voices that we most easily reach one another, and it is through the Word that God calls us. Raising our own voices to God in the prayer of the liturgy attunes our voices to God's, thereby training us to be one with Christ in ordering and restoring creation.

---

[182] For each of the following points, see "The Gift of the Living Tradition," Paul Jernberg, November 14, 2019, https://www.paul jernberg.com/new-blog/2019/the-gift-of-the-living-tradition.

[183] *Sacrosanctum Concilium*, no. 121.

Third, it "clearly announces, through its modes, melodic figures, and rhythms, that its purpose is sacred rather than secular, i.e., that we are being called to encounter God with profound reverence, rather than casually approach a mundane activity or event." As noted above, one of the chief difficulties with many attempts at hymnody today is that they have too close a similarity to popular music. Sacred music signals to us by its formal characteristics that it is, in fact, sacred—something set apart for God.

Fourth, it "maintains a certain modesty of form, so as to always point beyond itself to the Divine worship and communion which it is meant to facilitate." By attending to God's Word as the source of its content, true music also attunes us to reality. Sacred music praises God's glory and recognizes the vast gulf that lies between God's perfection and man's infirmity. This sobering reality, far from steeping us in despair, should cause those of us who gaze on the Cross to rejoice in God's loving-kindness. And, contrary to sloth, it should inspire in us a love for the created order and in particular for the Creator who is Himself our proper end.

Fifth, it has a "universal quality," such that it can resonate with people of many cultural backgrounds. Sacred music has the capacity to work across space and time. It works against the distension wrought by sloth.

Sixth, it should be "done with appropriate style and humble skill." These are qualities attainable by a broad spectrum of people, thus helping to foster active participation.

Seventh, it is "done with depth of spirituality and virtue." Again, sacred music is no mere sideshow to the liturgy. Rather, it gives flesh and body to the liturgy and ought to welcome those who hear it into the mystical and moral depth of the celebration.

Praise of the Creator who has lavished us with His love should bear that love in its very structure. Our liturgical music should not simply echo our pop hits. Rather, it should strive by its very form to resemble the glory of the one who has made us for Himself, and it should foster active participation. In this way, it welcomes us into that eternal liturgy being sung in Heaven and trains us to sing that liturgy throughout our temporal lives.

Cultural Variety

Much of what we have said on music to this point is prescriptive, following the guidance of the Church in the West. Yet, as *Sacrosanctum Concilium* hints, room should be made for the presence of other artistic traditions wherever they foster true devotion: "In certain parts of the world, especially mission lands, there are peoples who have their own musical traditions, and these play a great part in their religious and social life. For this reason, due importance is to be attached to their music, and a suitable place is to be given to it, not only in forming their attitude toward religion, but also in adapting worship to their native genius."[184]

In our day, as indeed during much of the nineteenth century, it is quite reasonable to speak of Europe and America as mission lands, places so far post-Christian that they stand as much in need of evangelization as, say, the Slavs of Sts. Cyril and Methodius. For true liturgy to arise in mission lands, it is critical that the liturgy, like all authentic festivity, incorporate the real feeling of the people, not imposing a cultural structure from above but sowing the local culture with the Church's universal culture so that the work of the people may be their work indeed.

In New Orleans, for example, there are several deeply fervent black Catholic parishes. The gospel hymns sung at their Masses, though far from chant, nonetheless present the joyous cries of

---

[184] *Sacrosanctum Concilium*, no. 119.

those who, with Israel, look to God for deliverance and turn to Him in thanksgiving and praise. The eucharistic character of the communion displayed in such song is evidenced by the missionary zeal of the people, demonstrated most immediately in the immense joy with which they greet strangers, welcoming them to a community which gives abundant witness to the power of Christ in its shared life.

What, then, shall we say in the last place about sacred music? Is it essential, for the sake of restoring Sunday, to employ only chant, polyphony, and traditional hymns? The long witness of the Church in the West testifies to the power of these forms, and yet the development of local culture would seem to demand admission of a broader variety of styles, for a Church that becomes all things to all men in order that a few might be saved. While we hesitate to rely too easily on Horace's dictum *"De gustibus non disputandam est,"* that is, "There can be no dispute with regard to taste," we ought not to leave sacred music purely to our sense of taste. The worship God demanded at Sinai was not a matter of the people's taste but of God's. All the same, God called forth what the people had concretely in their possession for His worship, and this pattern may fairly be applied to His calling forth the treasures of all cultures.

And indeed, Pentecost itself gives witness to the power of Christ to deliver the same message in an abundance of tongues. For it was not that those gathered in Jerusalem that day suddenly heard one common language, but rather "each one heard them speaking in his own language" (Acts 2:6). Babel is not merely undone. Rather, through the Spirit, all languages are harmonized to the language of the Word, able to hear the good news. The same possibility exists where music is concerned, with the variety of our musical languages capable of bearing the gospel.

By song we redeem time. Yet all song rests on the silence in which time flows from eternity. And so, aware of the irony in saying something about silence, we turn next to that very topic, that desert in which we learn truly to worship and in which we prepare ourselves for the Lord's Day and bear the Lord's Day with us through the week.

7

Silence: The Ground of Music and the Ground of Prayer

A holy priest has often described for me the early stirrings of religious awe that he felt in seeing his father kneeling in prayer in the night. There, beside the marriage bed, my friend imagines, his father strove with the many anxieties of the day, its labors and the many challenges which came with raising nearly a dozen children. It was perhaps then alone, in the night, when the children were mostly abed, that he could find silence in which to retreat to the inner desert of the soul where God awaits us.

Bl. Francis Xavier Seelos, himself a joyful ascetic, similarly described his experience of rising in the night and finding, no matter the hour, his superior, St. John Henry Neumann, on his knees in prayer. Both men derived the immense strength needed for their fasts, their long hours in the confessional, and their sleepless nights from communion with the Lord in the nocturnal silence of the heart. Both followed the example of the Divine Master, who Himself withdrew from the clamor of the crowds to the desert and to the high places where He could attend more intimately, in the midst of His human exertions, to His divine union with the Father.

RESTORING THE LORD'S DAY

All of our art, our architecture, and our music, all of our grand-est exertions in the celebration of the liturgy, have as their end the union of the soul with God in the Beatific Vision, and this vision beckons us into the eternal silence of the Trinity. We glimpse this silence for a moment in Revelation, at the breaking of the seventh seal, when all of Heaven falls silent for half an hour (8:1–2). We have lowlier, if still epic, experiences of such silence in, for instance, the conclusion of Dante's *Divine Comedy*, when the fourteen thou-sand lines of song conclude in the silence of the finite mind before the infinite good. We feel it as the last notes of Handel's *Messiah* shimmer and fade to quiescence. We taste it in the deep reflection which follows reception of Communion, when the Lord Himself enters the deserts of our heart and stills our being.

One of the Church's greatest gifts to the world is a tradition of silence, a tradition most awfully instituted at Christ's falling silent on the Cross and resting in the Sabbath silence of the tomb, a tradition which bore St. Anthony out to the desert, St. Bruno to La Grande Chartreuse, and Ven. Fulton Sheen to his holy hour at the outset of each day's labors. It is in silence, as on Mount Horeb, that God reveals Himself to Elijah, and it is in silence that we begin to detect the voice of God which thrills in the desert depths of the heart.

Our own world is in thrall to noise. Alarm clocks shriek us into anxious waking. Electric razors hum, frying pans clatter, and air conditioners kick clangorously on. Cars honk, brakes squeal, pundits drone. Music throbs in tune with our most bestial desires. And the noise, we could argue, is not simply audible. Obstacles to quiet, which is not itself silence but is at least a precondition therefor, are thrown at every moment before our eyes. The vast white noise of the Internet scrolls past our numb vision as we try to while away the hours till the end of the day, the end of the week, the end of the year, hoping each end will bring some measure of an anodyne. Hell itself, in Dante's conception, is filled with "shrieks, complaints, and deep cries" along with "odd tongues, horrid speeches, / words of pain, anger's accents, / voices deep and faint, and sounds of hands slapping."[185]

In all this, God remains silent. Indeed, the silence of God often becomes an indictment shrieked against Him. Where, we shout, is God? If God is real, why doesn't He announce Himself? Why isn't God speaking to us? Why has His Spirit ceased to guide us? (Hopefully this range of questions will suggest that the clamor is not only on the side of the secularist but also reverberates within the Church.)

We have become, as a culture—both secular and Catholic—inveterate talkers. And while speech is a mark of man, it is not our speech that defines us but rather our capacity to listen to the silence which is God's voice. We can imagine the silence in which Abraham sat at the door of his tent and saw the three strangers. We can feel the silence into which Noah must have withdrawn in order to hear God's call in a world gone badly wrong. And yet we are obsessed with talking. Day after day we are bombarded with articles, podcast episodes, and YouTube videos shouting out the evils of the world so that evil after evil sails through the technological void we have opened in our midst. Page after page of text, hour after hour of audio tells us ad nauseam just how bad we are and how to fix it. (Again, I note the irony of the utterance.) Yet we ought to consider closely just how much we allow ourselves to attend to God's voice. Are we obsessed with declaiming the many means by which we might once again offer worship to God? Or are we willing to go into the desert, bringing ourselves, our spouses,

---

[185] Dante, *Inferno* 3.22, 25-27.

our children, and our treasure, to wait quietly at the foot of the mountain for the Lord to tell us anew how to honor Him?

One of the marks of sloth is clamor. We recall the manner in which sloth drove Cassian's desert monks from their cells in search of conversation. And Cardinal Sarah refers us to Pascal: "How much of the evil of man's life derives from his inability to remain in his chamber."[186] By our endless divertissements, we prevent ourselves from experiencing the silence into which God desires to speak. Drawn out into frivolous conversation, or even into fruitful conversation which is nonetheless a distraction from the real work of the interior life, we shy away from encounter with the God who resides in silence within us.

We defeat sloth by withdrawing into the silence where we learn to speak with God's voice. That is, made one with Christ through the eucharistic liturgy, we hail the Lord enthroned within us and thus learn the real music of the Word—the one Word that the Father speaks from all eternity, the Word through whom all that is was made and redeemed. Learning this language, we come to rejoice in the concrete circumstances of life so repugnant to acedia. The silence wherein we attend the Lord within, the one who casts out the inner pharaoh, becomes the means whereby we live the joy of the Lord's Day through all days, remembering that This Day, the one the Lord has made, is the eternal now into which we are called.

Personal prayer, then, is the habit of attending to God in silence that shakes off sloth and allows us to advance from strength to strength, recognizing the Word in all creation and living in the joy of the Resurrection so that we, like the apostles, may be transformed and become capable of those works that evidence the Lord's work within us.

---

[186] See Sarah, *Power of Silence*, 33.

It is not enough, in short, to rest once a week in the quiet of the Lord's Day. We must rather be formed so as to bear the silence of the Lord's voice into every area of life, bringing about the Kingdom on earth and beating the death knell of those hellish gates which will not prevail.

What is perhaps especially difficult about the pursuit of personal prayer, of that intimate communion with the Father into which Christ Himself withdrew, is that in pursuing silence we will often be afflicted by the same feelings as those brought about by the noonday devil. For while sloth prompts us to reject divine charity and feel a deep distaste for everything around us, the way of purgation demanded by prayer will also lead us into the intense aridity of the desert.

Put otherwise, the passage of the soul into ever-deeper communion with God, and so into ever-deeper living of the Lord's Day, involves precisely entering into that utter abandonment, that profound divine silence, which Christ met with in Gethsemane and into which He cried, "My God, my God, why have you forsaken me?" (Matt. 27:46). The life of prayer demands a life of entry, not into the warm feeling of God's presence, but rather into that very feeling of absence that prompts so many in our woebegone world to cry out that there is no God. This process, by which we let go of ourselves in favor of Christ, allows us to exchange our earthly temporal anxiety for true Christian anxiety, which spends itself to the utmost in going after the lost sheep, which gives all in rejoicing over the found coin, which dies to self that others might have life. This journey to the heart of the Cross is the only one that affords the joy of the Resurrection, and its practice involves not simply forming a habit of verbal prayer but rather of going into the silence of our deepest interiority, that true inner room to which Christ directs us for authentic prayer, that we might there listen to the voice of the Father which breathes to us gently in the beating of our hearts and the flowing of our blood and all the other manifestations of that creative love that maintains the world in being.

This way is one that leads into that dark night so well described by Sts. John of the Cross and Teresa of Ávila, by Sts. Thérèse of Lisieux and Teresa of Calcutta. It is a way of purgation, of shutting out the world's light, not as evil in itself but as dimming that light beyond light whereby God diffuses His radiance to us. Again, it is critical for our present consideration that we compare the way the soul experiences the dark night—that is, as privation, as abandonment, as the profound absence of that radiant feeling of God's presence which so often spurs the fresh soul on to greater zeal—to the manner in which the soul experiences sloth. The soul oppressed by sloth, rejecting the will of God, makes itself a stranger to God's presence and so falls into a sickly sadness. The soul which goes the way of privation, on the other hand, advances for the sake of love and not for any emotional or sense-based feeling of that love, and so grows more and more attuned to the will of the Father and the real love of the Son, who hands on the love of the Father without the need to grasp the consolations of that love for Himself.

This can only happen in silence, which is, again, not simply quiet. Though silence requires forgoing the word's noise, the world's false visions of grandeur, honor, and pleasure, it above all entails the way of ascesis. Just as Christ, having been baptized, goes into the desert, into prayer, into fasting, so the soul that seeks silence must find not simply the quiet of the desert but rather the stillness of the appetites and of the passions, the stillness that permits the soul to hear the silent voice of the Father. Having walked the dark road of purgation, we become capable of that constant prayer to which St. Paul urged us, capable in the midst of the greatest noise of withdrawing into our inner room, shutting the door, and gazing on the burning of the Father's face.

Silence thus quiets the voice of sloth, which urges us, "Run! Go away! Find that far off place where you might finally be fruitful!" The whispering of sloth must surely have followed Christ, insinuating—so ineffectually, of course—that he had only to leave, to abandon the vulgar herd to their slaughter. Achilles, the demigod, heard the call of a peaceful life far from the wars of lesser men. He could simply have withdrawn into his great strength. And the demonic clangor would have risen to a new hellish crescendo had Christ, leaving the Last Supper, simply followed the road past Gethsemane to Bethany. But the immense silence Christ carried with Him bore Him on to further prayer, to the sanguine sweat which rolled in silence down His cheeks and into His beard even as the voice of the Father maintained its own awful silence. The same zeal for this divine silence whereby Christ had driven the moneychangers with their steady golden roar from the Temple led him to the Cross, where he instituted the new temple in His body. We, the members of this Body, in reception of the Body and Blood, are called with Christ into the silence of the Cross, the silence of the tomb, and the silence of eternity. Only from this silence can we speak the Word that charity demands ever more earnestly in our clamoring world.

In this way, too, we find that silence is essential to the liturgy and to the bearing of the effect of the liturgical action into every moment of life, so that, contrary to sloth, which yanks this way and that beneath the yoke of time, we may be delicately gathered up, as it were, to the bosom of eternity. The more deeply we enter into silence, the more we become capable of offering Christ Himself, with our own selves lain upon His breast, to the Father, becoming one with the only sacrifice that can avail us for salvation. In this silence, we begin to understand more deeply the impulse that drove the worshippers of Moloch to human sacrifice. In casting about for something worthy to propitiate the gods, man can find nothing more worthy on earth than himself. Yet what makes man worthy is not the body alone, which he shares with the plants and the animals, but rather the spirit breathed into man in the beginning. The body itself can thus only become a true sacrifice when it becomes the altar on which the mind and soul of man, his heart, the center of his being where God dwells, can be offered up to God as well. And only God Himself could speak the Word which, taking flesh, could put death to death and make man's sacrifice efficacious.

Cultivating Silence

How, then, can we cultivate this silence of contemplation? We do so in the first place by authentic celebration of the liturgy, which founds our noisy earthly journey on the silence of the love that is the Trinity. Nourished by Christ's Body and Blood, we can then cultivate silence through personal prayer and works of charity, as well as through contemplation of art and nature.

Jesus' Paschal Mystery ushered in a new era of worship, one in which worship expands beyond the walls of the Temple and into the realm of spirit and truth. With this marvelous expansion of the possibilities of worship, however, wherein we ourselves become tabernacles, comes the danger that we lose sight of the sacredness of our commission. Worshipping in spirit and truth does not mean worshipping as we see fit, a formula which ultimately means we will worship nothing, or, at best, ourselves. We must rather learn to worship in the Holy Spirit, in the Word who is the Truth, so that in them we are born into the life of the Trinity.

Cultivation of such worship, while freed from prescriptions of time and space, nonetheless demands training in making time and space sacred. Our personal prayer lives depend on carving out places and times dedicated to prayer and prayer alone. The Church has for centuries inculcated this practice through the Liturgy of the Hours, the Divine Office, which, by sanctifying certain hours, sanctifies all time in turn. While most Americans are little able to pray the Office entire, it is critical that we establish specific times each day for prayer. We tend to excuse ourselves from this practice, saying that our work is our prayer or that we simply don't have time, between work and children and rest, to pray. On the contrary, if our work and our rest and our raising children are to be fruitful, they must be founded on prayer, and the prudential judgment whereby we navigate the exigencies of daily life must be formed by a personal encounter with the Lord. As Mother Teresa admonished a young priest, even daily Mass and a daily Rosary and the Office were not enough for full flourishing in his vocation. We should even be willing, as she went on in a striking turn of phrase, to follow Christ in sacrificing charity itself to prayer.

We must, then, make time for prayer, a practice which typically involves designating a special place for prayer as well, whether a quiet room in the house, or an adoration chapel, or the like. In order to make these places truly sacred, we must ensure that the noise of daily life does not intrude. Most important, perhaps, we must have time away from screens, especially mobile devices, which constantly buzz, glow, and ring for our attention. How can we pray when we are wondering who just texted us, or when we are tempted to leave off prayer in favor of mindless scrolling through the doldrums of social media?

Developing habits of prayer can, in turn, demand that we give up those things that prevent our forming such habits. If we cannot put down our smartphones, let us get rid of them. If we cannot turn off Netflix, let us sell our televisions and give the money to the poor. If Facebook and Twitter persist in distracting us, let us delete our accounts. The more we say, "I couldn't possibly do that" of any of these measures, the more likely it is that we must we do them if we are to grow in our capacity for silence.

Likely—if we work during the day, and if we have children, and if we have committed ourselves to other labors besides—we will indeed find that making time for prayer demands prayer by night. Though our modern urban existence has gone far toward obliterating night and the quiet of rest, night often remains the best opportunity for most of us to devote time and space to the Lord. Prayer by night, the saints tell us, is indeed more efficacious than prayer by day, as it demands our vigilance, our renunciation of sleep and the other pleasures the night affords.[187]

By setting aside technology and our labors, by dedicating times and places to prayer,[188] and by committing ourselves to the purgative way which frees us from the attachments of the senses and even the spirit, we learn to live in the silence at the heart of the liturgy. This, in turn, prepares us for the labors of charity which, properly engaged, will lead us into deeper contemplative silence.

Mother Teresa often said that she would have been utterly unable to carry out her work for the poor of Calcutta without three to four hours of silent prayer each morning. It is likely that she thus spent more time in prayer each day than many of us spend in a week. And though we recall Gervase Crouchback's admonition that, in the spiritual life, quantitative judgments don't apply, we can probably find at least this quantitative difference between most of us and the saints, between those steeped in sloth and

[187] Ibid., 41.
[188] Ibid., 55.

those who have fully embarked upon the way of life: the latter pray a great deal more.

Such prayer is not a matter of simple leisure. Contemplation, far from being a matter of repose, constitutes in fact the highest human activity. The divine empyrean, the high Heaven of God's deepest dwelling, is in Dante's cosmos the place of highest activity, and our approach to God is a flight from the icy satanic center of things to the edge beyond which lives eternity. We see the height of this activity in Jesus' practice of withdrawing to a mountain to pray. Those on the mountaintop are moving faster than those at ground level. This high activity of prayer is not a luxury, either, for those who have nothing better to do. Rather, there is nothing better that any of us can do than to enter into communion with God. Just as the labor of Christ was founded on His union with the Father, so the work of a Mother Teresa demands digging deep into the interior desert to strike that well of living water.[189]

This was, Mother Teresa said, a practical necessity in her work. The poor will take all that we have. Having nothing, they will take anything they can from us. Far from the saccharine, heartwarming meeting with the noble poor of the human race which many of us imagine charity to be, any true gift of ourselves to the poor demands that we first root ourselves in Christ. We must be prepared, through waiting in silence, to give the living water that Christ gave to the Samaritan woman at the well.

True silence prompts works of charity, and true works of charity drive us back to silence, from which we take solace and nourishment. Through silence more generally, all of our faculties are hierarchically harmonized so that we become more capable of choosing the good in all aspects of life. The noise of the world

[189] Ibid., 47.

seeks to submerge our being into one plane of mediocrity, bidding us to listen constantly to podcasts and pop charts, to soothe ourselves with alcohol and drugs, to indulge our sexual appetites and occult curiosities. The life of silence demands calm, sobriety, and temperance, and it leads us into that unity of being that abides in God Himself.

Our journey into silence is a journey toward the voice of God. The way is fraught with the whisperings of other voices, and so the life of silence usually demands accompaniment by a wise guide. Sts. Teresa and John advert again and again to the importance of finding a good spiritual director if we wish to advance in the life of prayer, and certainly we should avail ourselves of holy guides who themselves go the way of contemplation if we wish to enter that silence which shines the light of the eighth day on all of our time.

Good art can also train us in silence. Beauty does not proceed from noisy activity but rather from quiet contemplation. The sculptor, the painter, and the poet are struck with inspiration in silence, and their work proceeds in silence. To appreciate such works itself demands silence, as the very quiet of art museums, of audiences in symphony halls, and even of libraries attests. A work of beauty is one that has necessarily grasped something of God, and its contemplation leads us to an encounter with the Beautiful One in turn—but only if we meet the work in silence, not as one who would surprise the hidden meanings of the thing or even interrogate the work, wresting value from it by our own intelligence. Rather, beauty stills us and, to the degree that it brings us into the presence of God, says, "You must change your life,"[190] reinforcing

---

[190] Rainer Maria Rilke, "Archaic Torso of Apollo," Poets.org, https://poets.org/poem/archaic-torso-apollo.

that unity of silence and charity, of worship and works of mercy, of the seventh-day rest in delighted contemplation and the eighth-day resurrection in glory. Moreover, that distension of the mind which plagues our age and which forms a key weapon in acedia's arsenal is put to flight by attention to a work of beauty. In allowing ourselves to be touched by an artist's work, we give ourselves up to an aesthetic contemplation which, though extended in time and space, trains us to experience that extension as flowing from eternity. True art, that is, drives out temporal anxiety, engrossing us so wholly that we scarcely feel time's passage and are indeed reminded of the truth that time is drawing us onward to an encounter with the eternal, an encounter so desired by Christ that He offers His blood for the sake of our being made ready.

As with art, we may readily turn to nature in seeking silence. Mother Teresa, in an oft-referenced passage, notes the way that nature proceeds in quiet.[191] The heavenly bodies wheel above us in silence. Trees grow for silent millennia. Babies form in silence in the womb. Even the sounds of nature could be said to proceed plainly from the silence of God's Word. Elijah does not, of course, hear God in the raging fire or in the storm or in the whirlwind, yet we can at least find clues to God's presence, sounds which point to silence, in the songs of birds and the rush of streams, in the high, lonely cries of gulls and the ache of the wolf's howl. In the sounds of nature, at the very least, we are brought up against things being what they are, fulfilling their nature in simplicity. Man, on the other hand, especially the man assaulted by sloth, hates what is simple. He seeks the complex as a counterpart to the variance of his inner faculties. He constructs false concepts, mental idols, which cater to his passions and conceal reality. Nature, on the

[191] See Sarah, *Power of Silence*, 34.

other hand, is always herself, and she lifts a mirror to us, showing us that we, too, are natural beings, albeit endowed with a nature that calls us beyond the bounds of material nature and into that immateriality which is, of all things, most real.

8

Noise Unlimited: The Program
of the Land without Sunday

At the outset of the eighth chapter of her book *Around the Year with the von Trapp Family*, Maria von Trapp recounts the most astonishing discovery of two Austrian neighbors on a trip to Soviet Russia. It was, the husband and wife said, a land without Sunday, one in which no church bells pealed their joyous strains across the quiet fields of morning, one in which the days of the week themselves had been abolished, with workers simply falling into grim rotations of work and leisure—nine days of work and one of rest, and so on. It was a land dedicated to labor, in which labor itself was the end.[192]

While we in contemporary America have not gone so far as the dissolution of the calendar week, we are nonetheless in many respects a land without Sunday. For many working Americans, the five-day work week is a bygone phenomenon. From grocery store employees to emergency room doctors, laborers in every sector of

---

[192] Maria Augusta von Trapp, *Around the Year with the von Trapp Family* (1955; repr., Manchester, NH: Sophia Institute Press, 2018), 167–168.

the American economy have grown used to being called on to work at all hours of the day and night. No time is sacred, and those who suggest otherwise often have an easy route to persecution for the sake of righteousness.

Indeed, von Trapp goes on to note the various shocks her family endured on relocating to America, from the strange silence of the church bells in New York City to the odd passion of the suburban rich for cutting their grass, washing their cars, and potting their geraniums, to the frank exclamations of one lady who, having been raised in a puritanical household where Sunday meant an inscrutable sermon and dull grownup talk on the porch, said she hated Sunday.[193] Sunday existed still as a calendar day, and people went to church—though often they arrived just in time, or a little late, sleeping in after a Saturday night's jollity—but this day was no longer the Lord's Day, a time ordered to the one who ordains all time. And, as the von Trapp family traveled, they found that this dissolution of the Lord's Day was spreading across the world, to the point that Pope Pius XII had to issue a call for a return to authentic worship. As the pontiff wrote,

> We see how the Christian people of today profane the after-noon of feast days; public places of amusement and public games are frequented in great numbers while the churches are not as full as they should be. All should come to our churches and there be taught the truth of the Catholic faith, sing the praises of God, be enriched with benediction of the blessed sacrament given by the priest and be strengthened with help from heaven against the adversities of this life.[194]

[193] Ibid. Consult also Laura Ingalls Wilder's *Little House on the Prairie*.

[194] Pope Pius XII, Encyclical Letter on the Sacred Liturgy *Mediator Dei* (November 20, 1947), no. 150.

The call, we have seen, was little heeded.

We have investigated many of the causes for this abnegation of the Lord's Day and the influence of acedia, focusing on the effects of the French, the industrial, the philosophical, the sexual, and the technological revolutions as turns away from being and hence from nature. We now consider in broader terms how these revolutions have shaped society and how the structure of society limits our capacity for liturgy. We will examine, first, the dominance of economy and its curious bifurcation of man as end in himself and man as obstacle through manipulation of language; second, the simultaneous exaltation and denigration of work; and third, the cheapening of sexuality as a tool to the destruction of the family.

Earlier we saw that *economy* means "law of life," and it is in this broad sense that we can speak of the economy of grace and the economy of salvation. In modern parlance, though, economy tends to refer simply to the monetary fabric of society, and money has indeed become the law of life. The desolation of the Lord's Day, whether through the state's reconstruction of time in Soviet Russia or materialistic apathy, as in the United States, points to the curious fact that, whether communist or capitalist, we have become, as a world-society, supremely concerned with material goods—who makes them, who owns them, and who benefits most from them.

This totalization of exchange as the measure of society can be traced in many respects to the influence of Marx, whose materialist reconfiguration of the Hegelian dialectic not only rejected the importance of the soul—and God—as the driving force in human affairs but also engendered in modern thinking a habit of viewing the world conceptually rather than personally. Bourgeoisie versus proletariat, capital versus labor, master versus slave—we have become accustomed thus to viewing the fundamental relations of men to one another. But this material conceptualization has perhaps served to reinforce a habit common to mankind: that of treating others under various conceptual rubrics rather than as persons. The pernicious influence of this habit may be seen in both liberal and conservative circles and, indeed, among a great many Catholics.[195]

Consider, for instance, the effect of hearing statements of the following kind: He is a liberal. She is a conservative. He is a Jesuit. She is a Nashville Dominican. He is a trad. She attends a novus ordo parish. He is gay. She is vegan. Such classifications, which allow for easy manipulation of classes of people through technologically powered advertising and political maneuvering, also allow us to comfortably write off those around us. For Christians, the danger is that we see the other not as a brother or sister, not as part of the eucharistic Body of Christ, at least in potentiality. Sloth delights in our seeing others this way, for, especially in an age in which the forces of sin may vaunt their advances upon the screens and airways of the world, it becomes ever easier for us to hate the concrete circumstances in which we find ourselves and so to reject God's will that we evangelize those His providence has entrusted to us.

The Left has shown itself to be particularly adept in its control of concepts through language, of course. By establishing a system in which the structures of power work actively for the oppression of certain classes, the Left defines the good and allows itself to become virtuous by fiat.[196] In this way, those who vocalize support of gay marriage, critical race theory, and transgender ideology establish their credentials as good people and acquire the power

[195] See Roger Scruton, *Fools, Frauds, and Firebrands: Thinkers of the New Left* (London: Bloomsbury, 2015), 8.
[196] Ibid., 11–13.

to despise those who disagree. This is especially dangerous when allied, as it is on the Left, with a general disregard for the principle of noncontradiction. We have entered dangerous territory indeed when people hold that it is true to say, simultaneously, that men can have children, that only those who have a uterus can have an opinion on abortion, and that you are a woman if you feel like a woman. The protean mind can brook no disagreement because it can have no conversation, having abandoned language as meaningful. This is an affront to the Logos and a coup for sloth and its detestation of the real order of things.

While Marx's dialectic has facilitated this conceptual treatment of others, it has simultaneously promoted the view, consonant with Sartre's existential individualism, that man is an end in himself. Our age is one which celebrates the individual, encouraging him to carve out his happiness by whatever means accord with his own definition of himself. Thus, we arrive in a society in which every member is obsessed with finding himself and then delivering an image of that self, via social media, to the rest of a society—which is, in turn, looking for self-fulfillment. Again, sloth rejoices, watching as we make ends of ourselves rather than looking to God as our telos.

Our obsession with concepts and with the self that conceives of itself as a unique end thus derive from the same error; namely, the failure to understand the self, and all other selves, in relation to Christ, who, by His love of the Father and entry into the world, establishes the pattern for all identity and difference: the trinitarian love that mysteriously unites three Persons. Only when we recognize the Trinity as our source and our end can we order ourselves properly to God, to ourselves, and to others. Only by giving ourselves up to the summons of the trinitarian love can we begin to live eucharistically, shaking off sloth by receiving God in the liturgy and by going from the liturgy on the mission of extending the trinitarian love to the world. Only by understanding ourselves as creatures who, through union with Christ and by our very bodily and spiritual makeup represent a cross-section of all of being, can we begin to understand what it is to treat man as an end, properly speaking. Man is an end because God loves him, not because there is no God.

The modern corruption of understanding of the self plays an even more critical role in destroying the Lord's Day in the way it affects our relation to work, whether in a labor-state like the Soviet Union, in which work became an end in itself, or in a consumer society like ours, which views work as a means to the definition of self whereby we measure happiness.[197] Jobs provide status, and they also provide money for the pursuit of entertainment, diversion, travel, and pleasure. Thus, we give ourselves over to work as the means of securing our happiness through material acquisition, and the whole structure of American society becomes founded on this process. We attend the best schools so that we can get the best jobs so that we can make the most money and retire and die. This is not to say that we are all miserable in our work. Nearly 50 percent of Americans report general satisfaction with their jobs, with the figure increasing above certain income thresholds.[198] But the focus of life is reduced to the horizontal plane, and, the transcendental having been evacuated, we begin to wonder just what we're meant to do with ourselves on Sundays. Or, in Daisy Buchanan's bewildered exclamation, "What will we do

---

[197] Pieper, *In Tune with the World*, 59.

[198] "How Americans View Their Jobs," Pew Research Center, October 6, 2016, https://www.pewresearch.org/social-trends/2016/10/06/3-how-americans-view-their-jobs/.

with ourselves today and this summer and the rest of our lives?"[199] What we do, as Pope Pius XII noted, is to give ourselves over to entertainment, to the pursuit of personal satisfaction rather than worship and mission.

The modern American view of labor can well be contrasted with that revealed in the early Church. There, labor was in the service of the gospel, with work of all sorts ennobled by such service. In the Gospel of Matthew, for instance, shortly after Jesus' Transfiguration, those who collect the Temple tax ask Jesus why He and His followers do not pay the tax, and Jesus, having discussed the matter with them, sends Peter to catch a fish, in whose mouth he will find a coin to pay the tax for both of them (Matt. 17:24-27). In Christ, our labor is transfigured such that it can fulfill the needs of man and, in turn, the needs of God on earth.

We see, too, in the Acts of the Apostles, the testimony that everyone brought the proceeds of his labor and the sale of his goods to the apostles, who, in turn, distributed according to need (4:34-35). Likewise, St. Paul dedicated himself to labor in whatever community he found himself, that he might not be a drain on the community and that he might preach by example as well as by word. He also prescribed faithful execution of our labor as an antidote to gossip and obsession with others' business (2 Thess. 3:12). All work may be transfigured, may become fruitful for salvation, when it is dedicated to God and performed in quiet faith.

Work, then, is not a necessary evil or a simple means to self-fulfillment according to our own designs. Rather, it is a divine commission to share in the creative labor with which, as Christ says, from the beginning until now the Father is at work.[200] It is

[199] Fitzgerald, *Great Gatsby*.
[200] Snell, *Acedia and Its Discontents*, 38.

also an invitation to silence of the sort that Christ entered in the hidden years, laboring faithfully, we suppose, alongside Joseph.

The modern system of work goes hand in hand with a sexual milieu that tends to the destruction of the family. Just as we pursue careers that allow us to shape our lives as we see fit, we also pursue forms of sexual expression that assert our own identity. This form of sexuality is dependent on the severance of the sexual act from its end. In his book *Cheap Sex*, Mark Regnerus points out how effectively the advent of the pill and abortion has cheapened sex, making it easier for men to acquire it without any substantial self-investment. And indeed, we have seen already that the sexual revolution has proven one of the most effective weapons at acedia's disposal. Contraception and abortion are powerful means to the rejection of the concrete reality around us, the state of being through which God prompts us to love and to allow ourselves to be more truly loved. The rage against any restrictions on abortion is a rage of acedia, a refusal to submit to the goodness of reality.

This state of affairs seems little likely to change for the better. Indeed, the change in American social life seems to be one of rapid decay. Nonetheless, we ought to consider those means whereby the ship of society might at least be driven before the storm until such time as we can turn and pull for pleasant harbors.

Toward the Good Society

What steps, then, can be taken to alter the shape of society, the better to foster Lord's Day devotion? While changes should be implemented at every level of society, from government and corporations to schools and churches to families and individuals, the more radical change will always proceed from the lowest levels; that is, the element nearest the root. Nonetheless, we will here briefly consider those political and corporate changes that could best serve for the full recognition of man's nature and his end; in the next chapter, we will treat the family as the school of holiness.

The Role of Government

Government exists, or ought to, for the good of those governed. The best government is that which secures to its citizens the greatest possibility of human flourishing. As the Lord's Day, properly celebrated, constitutes the highest happiness available to man in this life, it stands to reason that the government would do well to foster such celebration. It may do so both by establishing such laws as will permit a culture of life to flourish and by prescriptions aimed at highlighting the radical importance of the Lord's Day.

On this count, we need hardly mention the importance of pro-life legislation. The recent overturning of *Roe v. Wade* presents a sound advance in this direction. The backlash against the *Dobbs* ruling demonstrates the critical importance of abortion and contraception to the modern milieu, which depends on performance of the sexual act as self-assertive rather than procreative and unitive. Sloth, despising the solidity of reality, the yoke of what is, seeks by abortion and contraception to free its adherents of that yoke. Good legislation, on the other hand, should carve along the joints of reality, urging citizens to recognize reality and their place in it as a means to achieving the good and, in turn, of legitimate self-realization. A key next step in cultivating a culture of life would be to enact legislation that would enshrine a right to life for unborn children in the Constitution. The Left, and sloth, are winning this battle at the moment, with same-sex marriage nearing greater legislative protection as of this writing. Laws—and legal definitions—that permit disregard for the solidity of being and allow man to shape himself according to his own image are gathering strength, much to the detriment of the

Lord's Day, which calls man to an encounter with himself at the deepest possible level.

It is tempting to recommend legislation that, in addition to promoting a general culture of life, also specifically regulates labor and corporations to ensure that pay is sufficient to support families and that all laborers have sufficient time for Sunday worship. Indeed, the Fair Labor Standards Act of 1938, which limited the standard workweek to forty-four hours, with an amendment that lowered the standard to forty hours two years later, seems a just step toward such an end. We have seen, however, that the man freed from labor does not necessarily turn his attention to worship, especially if he is not attentive to the voice of God which, as with the Israelites at Sinai, would indicate the proper means of worship. Worship has declined steeply since the Second World War, and any significant reversal seems unlikely, whatever labor laws or blue laws might be enforced.

In their own small way, blue laws of certain varieties may be among the most effective steps government can take toward fostering Lord's Day observance. I had the immense pleasure of living for five years in Arkansas. Having grown up in New Orleans, I was very surprised, on moving to Hot Springs, to find that alcohol sales were prohibited on Sundays. It's a mild measure, and a far cry from laws that would forbid businesses to open on Sundays at all. Such laws, impossible to pass in our political climate, would also frankly be ill-advised from the standpoint of prudence. As St. Thomas More, drawing on Cicero, reminds us in *Utopia*, it is folly either to abandon the ship of state in a storm or to attempt to steer straight to port. Rather, prudence dictates steering with the storm and turning for home once the fury of the sea has abated. Small measures can be directed at reminding the populace that Sunday is different from the other days of the week, that it is a day not for the simple rest from care that a beer or glass of wine can bring, but for resting in the contemplative joy of the Lord, who says it is good that the world exists. Such laws recall Flannery O'Connor's comment that people turn to drink when they "aren't conscious that God is immediately present."[201] And the liturgy, drawing back the veil between time and eternity, ought to give us the eyes of the Son, who receives the love of the Father and is Himself the beginning in whom all things are made and have their goodness.

Education

More to the purpose than legislation, because nearer to the formation of the individual, is education. In recent years, education has become ever more marked by emphasis on the horizontal dimension of man's life, the progression from school to university to workplace to retirement, as well as on propagandistic rhetoric aimed at inculcating the attitudes and biases of the Left. Thus, public education tends to dismiss God as the fiction least worthy of human notice, to prime children for sexual promiscuity through the elevation of contraception and abortion as keys to the advancement of women, and to promote doing more and having more rather than being more. School is no longer a haven of contemplative leisure but rather a hive of frenetic activity.

Education ought rather to teach our children to delight in the good, to assent to the true, and to be still before the beautiful. Schools should be awash in good books. Their halls should echo with good music and laughter. Students should learn to draw and to strike up the violin, to mold clay and to name the

---

[201] Quoted in Christine Flanagan, ed., *The Letters of Flannery O'Connor and Caroline Gordon* (Athens: University of Georgia Press, 2018), 139.

constellations, to run in open fields and gaze quietly upon a Rembrandt or a Botticelli. They should learn to pray. They should perform Shakespeare. In all these things, we learn to look at the world, at ourselves, and at others, to attempt to see them as they are, as they have been created by God, and not through the conceptual propagandistic lenses by which we are trained, liberal or conservative, to view things.

As Plato expresses it in the *Republic*, education ought to be that process of turning about, of redirecting the attention of the soul so that its capacity to receive the good can indeed be directed to goodness.[202] As Caldecott points out, this is surely one of the finest aspects of Plato's work, one in which his radiant thought aligns brilliantly with the Christian conception of man as good though in need of being turned toward goodness.[203] Christian education in particular ought to direct the senses, heart, and intellect of the learner toward goodness wherever it shines forth, training him to look with God on the vitality of a world created and redeemed.

Corporations and Good Work

If education is aimed primarily today at preparation for corporate life—that is, for taking one's place in the workaday world—then corporations, too, have a profound responsibility for qualifying their missions and employing their laborers in ways that promote human flourishing. Corporations should create opportunities for employees to perform good work, work that engages the individual at various levels and that seeks the good rather than profit. This, perhaps, is the chief dissonance that must be resolved if corporate life is to coincide with Christian life. It is not, as Adam Smith tells

---

[202] Plato, *Republic*, bk. 7, sec. 518c–d.
[203] Caldecott, *Not as the World Gives*, 10.

us, from the good will of the butcher or baker that we get our meat but from his desire for his own benefit. But Christian businesses must be motivated not by a desire for profit but by a desire to serve the world alongside Christ, whereas the commercial world of modern America leads too often into a zero-sum game of those who profit and those who are preyed upon.

The lure of riches, especially in a materialistic society, exerts so profound an influence over much of our decision-making that we have in many cases failed to notice it at all. As Ishmael muses, "The urbane activity with which a man receives money is really marvellous, considering that we so earnestly believe money to be the root of all earthly ills, and that on no account can a monied man enter heaven. Ah! how cheerfully we consign ourselves to perdition!"[204] Even a businessman who calls himself Christian may find himself hard-pressed to deal honestly with his customers and his employees when profit is at stake. Surely, he may find himself saying, that old lady can afford to pay too much for this car. Surely that customer won't notice if I don't include the paint protection as I said I would. Surely she won't be concerned if I include an extended service contract with her purchase, provided her monthly payment stays the same.

This need not be the case. Corporations can and do contribute to a culture of life by conforming to justice; that is, by giving each of their members and each of their clients his due. The way of overcharging and underdelivering, pleasing as it is to the bottom line, is inimical to a Christian economy. The greatest profit and the greatest good very often do not coincide.

Likewise, corporations must ensure that employees are paid a just wage, a wage on which one parent can reasonably support

[204] Herman Melville, *Moby Dick* (New York, Norton: 2002), 21.

a family, as St. John Paul II argued in *Centesimus Annus*.[205] The necessity—or, at the very least, the felt necessity—for both parents to work outside the home in order to support a family has contributed immensely to our cultural habit of viewing life solely in its horizontal, materialistic elements.

Then, too, corporations should do good work. Those who pursue profit by any means necessary, the good and productive alongside the debased, the frivolous, and the criminal, have arrayed themselves against a culture of life by encouraging men and women to forsake their dignity as God's fellow laborers and to become instead minions in pursuit of superfluous or simply scurrilous ends.[206]

Good work is not frantic after the fashion of acedia. It should not set people flying about from task to task, from screen to screen, without opportunity for reflection or fulfillment. Where it entails haste, it is the haste of zeal: the kind that made Elijah, alone and on foot, outstrip the chariot of Ahab; the kind that causes children, those constant beacons of wonder, to run wherever they are going.

Corporations must also learn to honor the Lord's Day by shutting their doors, offering up a day's profit with confidence in the God who supplied manna to Israel in the wilderness, allowing their employees to engage in that worship that is the end of human life and toward which all authentic labor tends. By way of that corporate unity, which is a mark of the Body of Christ, corporations may indeed work for the greater glory of God and for the salvation of souls, helping their employees and clients not only to thrive materially but also to grow in holiness.

---

[205] Pope John Paul II, *Centesimus Annus*, no. 8.

[206] Consider the bitter case of Mr. Bulstrode in George Eliot's *Middlemarch*.

To these corporate considerations could be added a call for a renovated vision of economy, one which turns a more biblical eye to our usual considerations of profit. We recall, for instance, the way in which the Sabbath of Israel was intimately connected to the concept of the Jubilee, the year in which slaves were freed, property redeemed, and debts forgiven. "At the end of every seven-year period," says Deuteronomy, "you shall have a remission of debts, and this is the manner of the remission. Creditors shall remit all claims on loans made to a neighbor, not pressing the neighbor, one who is kin, because the LORD's remission has been proclaimed" (Deut. 15:1-2). As the good reverend John Ames puts it in *Gilead*, "In Scripture, the one sufficient reason for the forgiveness of debt is simply the existence of debt."[207] Such a system is so foreign to our own way of relating to each other as to be unthinkable, and yet we ought to consider ways our economies might practically approach debt in a more charitable manner. Caldecott, for instance, emphasizes the success of the micro-loan system.[208] More radically, we ought to open our hearts to the individual opportunities we have to proclaim liberty to those around us, forgiving debts owed to us in a spirit of Lord's Day freedom.

Such an alteration of economies could likewise admit of a kind of generosity at the margins of labor that allows for the feeding of those at the margins. We recall the Deuteronomic provision for the poor in the prescriptions against gleaning to the very edges of the fields. Israel was to leave a kind of ragged edge to their fields—as to their garments—to be an unfinished space where God might continue His work of creation. Loving the Lord's Day anew calls us to allow such considerations to

[207] Marilynne Robinson, *Gilead* (New York: Picador, 2004), 161.
[208] Caldecott, *Not as the World Gives*, 69-71.

inform our business practices, finding those margins where we might provide for the poor.

Becoming Saints

The single greatest means for transformation of society is for men to become saints. Government programs, corporate policies, and educational practices should all conduce to the formation of good men and women who are open to the possibility of encounter with Christ, who recognize the goodness of the created order, and who share the work of Christ in redeeming that order. But hearts are most radically changed by the personal encounter with the redeemer of man, an encounter the saints can extend through the witness of Christ in their own bodies.

If we wish to change our society, to leaven it so that all may grow into one in Christ, we must become holy. We must avail ourselves of the liturgy, the source of our holiness as the locus of our encounter with the living God, and we must become truly alive so that those who encounter us will be drawn to the liturgy that enlivens us.

This is a difficult labor, the true labor that transforms all other labors: the cultivation of this piece of earth the Lord has entrusted to our care. We must undertake the labor with joy. And while our temperaments are not entirely ours to control, we should at least eschew a kind of dour pessimism that can only manage to bemoan the state of things. Certainly, we will face setbacks. We will face frequent loneliness in striving to find the narrow road. Yet, like the bit of yeast which falls into the darkness of the dough, separated from all its kind by what seems a vast, sticky void, or like the seed which falls into the earth and loses the light of the sun and the company of its own, we too must enter society, dying to ourselves, losing the comforting sight of our fellows as we go out among the lost, beckoning our fellows to the joy the Master has shared with us.

If the liturgy makes us saints in supereminent fashion, then it belongs to the family to teach us how to live liturgically, to train us in tasting the goodness of what God has given us, including Himself, our world, our fellow men, and ourselves. And so we turn now to our discussion of the family, our school of sanctity.

9

Family: The School of Sanctity

Jesus rejoiced in family life. Having grown up in the quiet joy of the Holy Family, He made it His practice to spend time among families during His public ministry as well, whether with the family celebrating a wedding at Cana, with the family of Simon Peter, or with the beloved family of Martha, Mary, and Lazarus. Indeed, it was with these last three that Christ chose to spend the last of His mortal Sabbaths. And so they give us a model of Lord's Day living, of honoring the Sabbath by inviting Christ into our midst, praying with Him, dining with Him, and lavishing our substance upon Him.

"The Christian family ... is the first community called to announce the Gospel to the human person during growth and to bring him or her, through a progressive education and catechesis, to full human and Christian maturity," writes John Paul II in *Familiaris Consortio*.[209] This community was willed by God from the beginning as a means for man, made in God's image and likeness,

---

[209] Pope John Paul II, Apostolic Exhortation on the Christian Family in the Modern World *Familiaris Consortio* (November 22, 1981), no. 2.

to participate more fully in the shared life of the Trinity. As R. J. Snell notes, the striking shift from God's repeated affirmation that the things of creation are good and indeed very good to His seeing that "it is not good ... that the man should be alone" signifies the profundity of the divine largesse.[210] The delight God takes in creation flows from the delight the Father takes in the Son, and therefore the delight a husband and wife take in each other—which is in part a final delight the Father takes in Himself—becomes a source of joy in all that is.

The family, in which love of husband and wife is embodied in the life of the child, provides a type or model of the Church. Just as Christ offered up His body and so allowed for sanctification of mankind in His Body, the Church—which was present at the foot of the Cross in the person of the mother from whom He derived His body—so husband and wife say to each other, "This is my body." Each offers his or her body to the other, and each, gazing with love upon the other, says, "This one, at last, is bone of my bones and flesh of my flesh" (Gen. 2:23). Likewise, each sees self and spouse in the body of the child. And just as the Church makes her members one in body through sharing of her body in the Eucharist, so a mother makes her family one in body through her own body, which receives the body of her husband and forms the body of the child. The family, that is, is itself eucharistic—not, of course, that the family is sufficient unto itself, apart from the sacraments. Yet the family is a form into which sacramental grace naturally flows.

Indeed, the connection between the family and the sacramental life of the Church is reinforced not only by the familial nature

---

[210] R. J. Snell, "Wasting Time Well: Leisure as the Point of Education" (lecture, New York University, September 21, 2022).

of Israel, the family of God descended at last from Adam, the son of God, but also by the importance of the domestic churches in the life of the early Church. These dwelling places, home to both families and the liturgy, cast vivid light upon the relationship between the life of the family and the life of the Church, both of which take their fundamental unity from that bodily incorporation that allowed Adam to see, at last, bone of his bone and flesh of his flesh.

The family, setting all men in immediate concrete relation to others, serves as a first defense against the tendency to deal with our fellow creatures under mere conceptual rubrics that convey value according to a particular worldview. In the family, we encounter first not man or woman or liberal or conservative, but mother and father, sister and brother. We encounter the other in terms of the most intimate relationships—relationships which, proceeding from the act of conjugal love, call for a response of love.

The family aids us in moving beyond the spheres of our own limited selves—spheres sloth loves for us to inhabit—by revealing us to ourselves in the other. We see this in God's process of finding a suitable mate for Adam. As God presents each of the animals to Adam, He invites Adam to give them names—to apply concepts to them. And though this use of words permits Adam a share in the creative power of God, it does not allow him the full scope of creative relationality afforded by recognizing the self in the other. It is only when he sees Eve that he is able to enter into the relationality by which he participates in the life of the Trinity, a relation that comprises the unity of self and other.

God wills us to be in relationship to one another, to love one another as He has loved us. In our selfish pursuit of our own ends, we tend instead to deal with others as mere instances of some concept that is either repugnant or useful to our fulfillment of our visions for ourselves. Sloth advances when we begin to see others as merely Republicans, Democrats, liberals, conservatives, and so on. When we understand others in this way, we give ourselves license to forgo the relationships God wills for us.

We find examples of this kind of dismissal throughout Scripture. It could be argued that we see it as early as Adam's complaint that "the woman" gave him the fruit to eat. In this instance, she becomes not his wife, flesh of his flesh, but rather the woman, the other who has led him into sin. In so rejecting Eve, Adam also rejects himself, putting away the relationship God has enjoined upon him.

An even keener example may be found in Luke 18, when Jesus delivers the parable of the Pharisee and the tax collector in the Temple:

> Two people went up to the temple area to pray; one was a Pharisee and the other was a tax collector. The Pharisee took up his position and spoke this prayer to himself, "O God, I thank you that I am not like the rest of humanity—greedy, dishonest, adulterous—or even like this tax collector. I fast twice a week, and I pay tithes on my whole income." But the tax collector stood off at a distance and would not even raise his eyes to heaven but beat his breast and prayed, "O God, be merciful to me a sinner." I tell you, the latter went home justified, not the former; for everyone who exalts himself will be humbled, and the one who humbles himself will be exalted. (10–14)

The Pharisee, instead of really praying by entering into relationship with God, merely prays to himself. Casting his eyes about, he rejoices that he is not like "this tax collector." (How often do we rejoice that we are not like that liberal, that woke propagandist, that moron?) The tax collector, addressing God, calls himself a sinner and so reflects rightly on his relationship to God and the world around him. He has violated the divine ordinance, and he asks for help from the only quarter possible.

The good family, cherishing the relationships entrusted to it by Providence, teaches us from an early age that love thrives not simply in the ways others are similar to us but precisely in the measure to which it can go out to those who are not like us. It is the son's being different from the father that allows the father to pour himself out in the self-gift that marks fatherhood. It is the old uncle's cantankerous nature that allows the weekly meal with him to become a moment of self-gift. It is a parent's failing body and mind that allow an adult child to make some return on that love which nourished him in infancy.

By its very nature, then, the family is, or ought to be, a school of holiness, a haven in which we learn proper love for others, a love that sees not conceptually but personally. We also learn love for ourselves that is founded on the love of a mother and father who are good to us and teach us the goodness of the Father—and love for God, who gives us His very body and makes us one with Him, just as mother and father give of their bodies. We are taught to rejoice in the concrete circumstances of our lives, to put off the slothful inclination to disdain the people and places among whom God has willed us to be. We are taught to labor well and to pray well, and to join the two by a constant contemplative presence to the God who is ever present to us, rejoicing in our existence.

In these several ways, the family trains us for our end in the heavenly liturgy, and if it is to do this well, then it must be ordered around the earthly liturgy whereby our salvation is wrought. And this is not easy. We have been speaking of family life in ideal terms, yet it is probable that our own families and those around us lead lives of a far different sort. We are constantly busy, rushing from homework assignment to late-night work e-mail to breakfast preparation to workout routine. We grumble at each other. We fight. We lose our tempers over looming bills. We get sick. We fail to communicate with each other and with the God who should ground us. Things fall apart, as Eve and Adam fell from God and from each other, as Cain fell from Abel, as the world fell from goodness before the Father brought the flood. The answer to the centrifugal force of sin is a family that orders itself properly to God, giving itself over to the familial bonds of covenant.

What, then, are the concrete steps whereby a family can orient itself toward liturgical living? To set out a specific program for that sort of family life which best attunes us to the heavenly liturgy is probably imprudent, for prudence is the art of bringing the universal to bear on the particulars of specific human decisions. Holy families, to depart slightly from Tolstoy, are all alike in setting themselves apart for God, yet they often differ in the specific manner of doing so. The life of Sts. Louis and Zélie Martin, parents of St. Thérèse of Lisieux, was quite different from that of St. Thomas More, which was again quite different from that of St. Katharine Drexel's parents. The Holy Family was itself a beautiful thing all its own.

While we cannot supply any specific guidelines for a universal program of holy family life, we can nonetheless describe a pattern of living that prepares the family members for the heavenly liturgy by attuning them to the divine life. This attunement could be said to proceed according to the transcendentals of unity, goodness, and truth. The liturgy makes us like God, makes us one, makes us good, and makes us true; the family that pursues these three things, and so becomes beautiful, is well on its way to holiness.

The Transcendentals as a Pattern of Family Life

God is one. And the intensity of His unity is made the more so by His being Trinity, by the relation of love which renders His unity expansive, radiant, and benevolent. We have noted how this unity is extended to mankind through the Church, which makes her members one in the very Body of Christ, and we have seen how the family follows the unity of the Church by the way man and wife are made one flesh, and the way children take a share in that flesh, through the nourishing, unitive powers of the mother.

At the most basic level, the unity of the family should endure through the unity of marriage and an overflowing marital love that invites the living response of the children. The mutual subordination of husbands and wives, modeled on the relationship between Christ and His Church, models for children the loving self-sacrifice upon which the Church is built up. It likewise mirrors the order of creation—the mother, who is honored as queen in her household, reflects the place of Eve as last of all created things, while the father, who labors for his family, represents Adam in his divine commission to till the land and keep it. Parents who honor their children teach the love of the Father, and children who honor their parents learn early to reverence the God who is our source and end. This unity is heightened when each member of a family performs his or her proper role. In any organization, from a family to an army to a particular organic body, unity comes about when all the members are directed toward their end through the direction of the highest part. Thus, all the members of an army are directed toward the end of victory by the general, whose orders guide the lieutenants, privates, and all the rest to do their specific duties. A corporation does its work best at the corporate level when good management directs all employees in every level to the proper execution of their roles. A family, which is intended for Heaven, best succeeds under mutual subordination—which is the legacy of Eden, of the Gospels, and of the letters of Paul. And all members are directed to God as their end.

The unity of the family faces constant attack in our day, though it should be noted that challenges to the family have plagued us since Eden. We see in the Holy Family, of course, a particularly potent response to the threats to this unity—threats that in many ways are directed against St. Joseph but that ask that all the family grow in wisdom and stature before the Lord. We can imagine the temptations to which St. Joseph was subject when he heard of Mary's pregnancy, the whispers as he passed through crowds, the worm of doubt in his mind. Again, we can sense the immense anxiety that rose against him in response to Herod's threat against the Christ Child's life, the hardship of the flight to Egypt, a flight that had so often proved perilous for Israel in the past. We feel with him and with Mary the agony of those hours without the young Christ when He dwelt in the Temple and taught with wisdom, and we ponder with all of them the mysteries of God's growth in human form. Through all, the good foster father protected his family, and, even after his death, he remained present to them: that carpenter who, as all knew, was Jesus' father.

The life of Mary in turn comprises an unfailing font of wonder. The Church has always seen in her the New Eve, and indeed, we can see that, in Mary, God can, as it were, rejoice as Adam did in the sight of Eve. For from Mary comes the very flesh of God. As the Second Vatican Council expresses the matter, "She is endowed with the high office and dignity of being the Mother of the Son of God, by which account she is also the beloved daughter of the

Father and the temple of the Holy Spirit."[211] In no other human save Christ Himself can we see the life of the Trinity so fully at work. And while the rest of mankind must have seemed in some way alien to her, free as she was from all stain of sin, she nonetheless offers to us a vision of humanity and of motherhood in which we can begin to see ourselves as we look toward her son for the full revelation of our humanity.[212] Hers is, as it were, like the light of the moon, which in the darkness of night or brilliance of day trains us to lift our eyes in hope to Heaven and strengthens us to look in time to the glorious Son, who is the lamp of the New Jerusalem.

Christ Himself, of course, models for us the kind of childhood that abides in holiness and proceeds to ever-deepening love of God and others. He is obedient to His parents. He works quietly alongside His earthly father, showing us that we need not look to far-off lands and glorious deeds to bring about the Kingdom. And when at length He gives Himself up to that most salutary death, He ensures that His mother is taken into St. John's home.

In all ways, the Holy Family models the unified orientation to Heaven that we so ardently crave and from which the world so noisily distracts us.

This orientation to God also demands a proper orientation to all subordinate goods. A family will struggle to serve God well if the mother or father is dedicated primarily to financial gain, the acquisition of power, or the pursuit of pleasure. All such goods

[211] Vatican Council II, Dogmatic Constitution on the Church *Lumen Gentium* (November 21, 1964), no. 53.

[212] On this matter, see Georges Bernanos, *Diary of a Country Priest* (Cambridge: Da Capo, 2002), 211: "Think what we must seem to her, we humans. Of course she hates sin, but after all she has never known it.... The eyes of Our Lady are the only real child eyes that have ever been raised to our shame and sorrow."

should be prized, understood, and used in the measure of their ability to help or hinder the family in its journey to God.

Doing the good and being united to the eternal goodness which is God depends in large part upon becoming virtuous. While it must be recognized that in the Christian life there are no set formulas for success—that Dismas, the Good Thief, was only good in respect of his dying wish and not as a result of a life of Aristotelian virtue—still the way of virtue is one of the most excellent means whereby a family may prepare its members for happiness in the Beatific Vision. A family should practice justice among its members, ensuring that each one receives his due and that the entire family gives of itself in the appropriate degree for the realization of a just society. Mothers and fathers should train their children in temperance with respect to food, drink, and even money. They should supply their children with models of fortitude in the face of the constant objections that modern living raises to virtue. And they, having imbibed the principles of a life ordered to God, should every day manifest prudence, choosing such concrete means as will bring the universal to bear on particular situations.

These cardinal virtues, of course, cannot be fully realized without the action of grace and the presence of those theological virtues of faith, hope, and charity which always begin in the gift of God and which alone allow a family to be good in the richest sense. The good works which St. James demands (James 2:14) are themselves not truly possible without faith, hope, and love. At the same time, the exertion of the will in the practice of the cardinal virtues helps to till the ground for the reception and germination of the theological virtues. The two constantly inform each other, fostering mutual development in light of that divine love toward which we tend as naturally as a flower to the sunlight.

In truth, we are inclined to goodness. And in being good, in becoming one with God, we must also become more true—true to the Father and true to the Word whereby we may be true to ourselves. A family cannot become holy unless it celebrates the truth. Being truthful involves speaking truthfully to one another, of course. It demands also that we eschew the false narratives modernity has placed before us: the tales of materialism, hedonism, and utter illogic which demand our complete allegiance or else call for our social exile or execution. It calls us to know the things of the world better, to learn the proper words for our thoughts, so that, by our language, we might unite ourselves more fully to the Word who is the beginning of all things and who brings all things to redemption.

The Holy Family, made one in the Logos-made-flesh, enjoyed in their son the presence of eternal truth, and they learned truth in the slow, silent years they shared. From the quiet of the manger in Bethlehem to the calm of the carpenter's shop, in the silent pondering of the words of Simeon and in reflection on Jesus' teaching in the Temple at age twelve, this family together mounted along the way of truth. Mary, Queen of Heaven, continues to direct us to the truth, telling us, "Do whatever he tells you," beckoning us to do the will of the Father and so to become Christ's mothers, brothers, and sisters. She holds the crucified body of the Truth in her arms, bidding us look with her on the one scourged for our sins, and nourishing the Church from the Upper Room till today, encouraging us to continue to walk in truth.

Truth, goodness, and unity align as well in beauty. And whether we treat beauty as itself a transcendental or consider it a kind of radiance, supervenient upon goodness, certainly we can aver that it is the experience of beauty which often most penetratingly testifies to the presence of truth and goodness. It is, to paraphrase

Benjamin Franklin on a rather different subject, a sign that God loves us and wants us to be happy.

The family should, then, be beautiful. This does not mean, of course, that the family should pursue that sort of meretricious beauty which the world champions, one founded on the lure of the eye and the greed of the heart. The beautiful family is the one that pleases by the order of its shared life. The beautiful family keeps a home where its members can thrive and where guests can be welcomed. It does so primarily through the mutual self-gift of father and mother and children, who perform the labors of the household for the sake of their love of Christ and each other. The beautiful family makes its neighbors feel more at home by its kindness and its generosity. The beautiful family shows the face of Christ to its sick children and elders, to its sons and fathers struggling with addiction, to its anxious and overburdened mothers.

Much of the work of bringing forth the beauty of family life lies in training ourselves in good taste. One of the greatest obstacles to love of the liturgy today is a scarcity of appreciation for beauty. Even if we build the most beautiful churches, sing the most beautiful chant, preach the most beautiful sermons, and surround ourselves with the most beautiful sacred art, we can little expect this beauty to reach a world which has dieted for decades on the vulgar, the obscene, the frenetic, and the vicious aesthetic. Generations raised on Taylor Swift and Kanye West often have little liking for Mozart. Those who enjoy the exploits of the Kardashians may be little equipped for delight in Homer and Dante. And those whose supreme pleasure is to watch television and eat wings may struggle to appreciate even the wonder of a Notre Dame or Chartres.

Families, then, should seek as much as possible to immerse themselves in beauty. Let them cultivate rose gardens and take excursions to the sea and to the forests. Let them read many good books and set orchids on the dinner table. Let them play the works of Bach and Palestrina as they get ready for the day, and let the children know from first youth the joy of making music. Let them dance and delight in each other. Let them hang icons, family photos, and other lovely images on their walls. Let them eat good food lovingly prepared, and all the better if they have grown, caught, killed, and cleaned it themselves. Let them tell stories around campfires. Let them read aloud and sing. Let them know what it is to be loved, and from this love to give forth that radiance that marks joy.

For the good family should give off a kind of radiance, should be marked by a kind of living that sets it apart from the world, that makes it holy. The beautiful family need not, of course, be the best dressed or the most elegant or the most current in home decor trends. The Holy Family was itself a poor one. Yet holy families in general live in such a way as to depart from the wide and easy way of the world and to draw others to desire the kind of life they lead. They inspire others to think to themselves, as beauty always makes us think, "You must change your life."

One of the most moving examples of a faith which renders family life beautiful, which causes a family to stand out from the world by a kind of graceful radiance, is to be found in Chaim Potok's *My Name Is Asher Lev*, the story of a young boy of tremendous artistic gifts born to a devout family of Orthodox Jews. Asher's New York City community, from his mother and father to his uncles to the rebbe, their religious leader, devote themselves tirelessly to the preparation of the world against the coming of the Savior. Asher's father travels relentlessly as the rebbe's emissary, while his mother devotes herself to doctoral studies and becomes, in time, a well-known scholar, completing the academic work her brother had begun before his untimely death. Asher's uncle, a jeweler, amasses a fortune, which finances many of the community's projects. And everyone abides by the rhythm of the Jewish year and, most of all, by the Sabbath—observance of which is not limited to an hour's pale attendance at church but which, rather, stretches from Friday evening, with its ritual baths, to Saturday morning in the synagogue and subsequent family gatherings devoted to discussion of the Torah. There is a sense, throughout the book, of the kind of urgency which ought to characterize all authentic human life. For the Jews of Potok's works, life is no simple, laborious march toward death, punctuated by weekends and capped by an idle retirement. For the Lev family and their community, life is instead constant preparation for the Messiah, with the Sabbath as the beating heart of time—time which, in its passing, bids us, "Be ready, be ready, be ready, He comes."

This readiness of Potok's Jews models for us a truth that Israel first learned in the desert. The Sabbath enjoined on God's people recalled God's rest in the beginning and anticipated Israel's rest in the land promised to them through Abraham. For the Jews who left Egypt, the Promised Land was but a generation away, with the River Jordan there at the end, like the river of time itself. Some made the crossing, while others, even Moses, merely sighted the land from afar, and others still were swallowed up in the desert of their own perfidy.

Paradise looms at the end of every generation. It is the land promised us not by way of the mortal son, Isaac, but by way of the immortal son: Jesus. As families, it belongs to us to remind each other of this promise and to urge each other on through the desert. As families, let us not worry about what we will wear or what we will eat—Israel ate in the desert, and his clothes and his shoes did not wear out. Let us instead be concerned with the veil torn once and for all when Christ hung upon the tree, and let us peer through that torn veil at the heavenly liturgy made present in every Mass.

We consider now, in our last chapter, what exactly we can do to keep the Lord's Day holy. That, of course, has been in some sense the concern of this entire book. Here, though, we hope to make a few practical recommendations by which the laity especially can make the day one of rest infused with the joy of the Resurrection.

10

Homo Vivens: The Lord's Day Regained

In the Mass, we encounter the Beginning and the End, the one who was and is and is to be. Encountering Him, our minds go back to the origin of time and forward to its fulfillment, to Genesis and to Revelation. And our memory and imagination, made one in the Eucharist with the realm of eternity, raise up our own past and future as an offering and allow our time to be transformed, permeated by the eternal love that sustains it.

In offering our time to eternity, we allow eternity to inform every moment of time, enabling us to learn to pray always, and so beginning to experience that presence of the Father which is the delight of Heaven. The Lord's Day is a gift that permits us to step away from the stream of workaday existence to drink at the font of being. It is a moment that bids us feast, in fulfillment of the Sabbath that was the first feast of Israel.

How, then, do we feast? What can we do to live the Lord's Day truly, basking in the divine radiance so that we, like Moses leading the people out of Egypt, become radiant ourselves?

Maria von Trapp again supplies us with an admirable model. In her family's native Austria, prior to World War II, it was the rule in rural areas, she says, for preparation for the Lord's Day to begin on Saturday night. When the week's labor was put away, the Sunday-best clothes were laid out, baths were had, and meals were prepared, something in the manner of the way we go about Christmas or New Year's Eve. For Austrian Catholics, though, this was not a time for parties or frivolity but for joyful preparation to receive the Lord. To that end, many people went to Confession Saturday evening as well, while those who could not went Sunday morning, when families, dressed in those clothes reserved for the occasion, attended Mass. After Mass were meals, songs, dances, and games, all dedicated to engagement with those others who had shared in the eucharistic feast.[213]

To us, such a celebration of Sunday seems almost dreamlike. Perhaps it strikes us as unreasonable, even impossible. Perhaps it attracts us, nearly even compels us to attempt it, but at the end of the day seems incompatible with our work-from-home, extracurricular-riddled, high-intensity lifestyles.

For the von Trapps, though, even this form of observance came to seem insufficient, proceeding as it did from simple tradition rather than from a movement of the heart. True liturgy always proceeds from the heart, and mere mechanism is antithetical to its nature. Thus, the family began to study the Lord's Day intently, seeking out the wisdom of their priest, that they might learn how Christians throughout the ages had feasted and how they might make the feast more their own. They began, like the Jews of Potok's novels, to encounter the Scriptures more actively. They read the Mass readings Saturday evening and discussed them by way of preparing their hearts to receive the Word. They dedicated themselves to an authentic celebration of the Eucharist, not simply because things were done that way, but because the very possibility

---

[213] Von Trapp, *Around the Year*, 168–170.

of salvation rested on the Eucharist. The Lord's Day meant not the rest of idleness, but rather the rest that is the greatest and most profound of human activities: the contemplative turning of the mind and heart to the God in whom they rest.

After Mass, the family still enjoyed a good meal with neighbors, and the children organized dances, games, and songs. And these festivities flowed not from a desire to while away free time but from the urge to celebrate the life-giving presence of the Lord on His day. To this spirit of prayerful play the family also added a commitment to performing works of mercy on the Lord's Day, with such works serving to allow a share in the merciful activity of the Father.[214] Thus, the whole experience of Sunday became not just a few sparse moments of rest, desperately seized from the jaws of the workweek. Rather, it became a moment of presence to the Lord, the presence that allows us in turn to be most present to ourselves and to those whom God has set before us, that we might rejoice in them, saying, "Yes! It is good that you are here!"

How can we today celebrate in this way? How can we keep the Lord's Day holy? While this book can provide no complete manual for Lord's Day observance, we can at least offer one guiding principle, along with suggestions for the sorts of activities to avoid and others to pursue on Sunday.

The principle is this: whatever we do on Sunday, we should be able, in doing it, to say with Jesus, "My Father is at work until now, so I am at work" (John 5:17). Any work, any activity, in which we are engaged on Sunday should only be the sort of work that belongs to the Father: creating and ordering, healing and restoring, loving and going out to those most in need of love.

---

[214] Ibid., 176.

With this in mind, let us consider first those things which are best left *undone* on Sunday.

How Not to Feast

In what follows, we wish to avoid casuistry — that is, we are looking to general rules and not to the extreme cases that might call for exceptions. If, for instance, a mother has just been left a widow without external means or family provision, and a second job that requires her to work on Sundays can stand between her children and starvation, we would do best, probably, not to begrudge her the job — and, if we have the means, to supply her with what she needs to obviate the need for the job in the first place. If a father has just lost his wife and finds himself home on Sunday at last, the funeral having been completed, with no food in the refrigerator or clean clothes in the dressers, his work of ordering and loving may well entail doing some laundry and getting some groceries, hopefully with the aid of family and friends. Again, though, these are extraordinary circumstances, whereas we are concerned with general norms for true Sunday festivity.

To begin, then, let us first be sure to put aside our work on Sundays. As employers, this demands giving our employees the day off and shutting our doors for the day, offering a day's profit as a sacrifice to the Lord and a vote of confidence in Providence. For employees, it requires staying home from the workplace, to be sure. But in this age of technology, it also involves leaving aside the laptop and smartphone and letting those e-mails wait until Monday. Let teachers leave off their grading and writers their writing. Let students set aside their homework. Let the business of the workweek be managed during the workweek. This may, of course, involve doing extra work on Friday or Saturday. The Israelites, too, had to collect a double portion of manna on the sixth day, but the payoff was the sweet, honeyed savor of true rest with the Lord.

Second, let us avoid chores on Sundays. Laundry, grocery shopping, cleaning, cutting the grass, washing the car, purchasing clothes, and balancing the checkbook should all be done on the other days of the week. Not only does this free us for the spiritual labor of the day, but it also helps to free those constrained to work from some of their labor. Again, this may require extra labor on Friday or Saturday. So be it. Such extra labor trains our hearts to prize the Lord's Day for what it is, and not for the opportunity it gives us to waste our Fridays and Saturdays in frivolous pleasure-seeking.

Third, let us stop "working for the weekend." As St. John Paul II points out, the cultural phenomenon of the weekend, brought about by reduced working hours and by a felt need for rest, nonetheless often dissolves into a spiritually fruitless span of idleness, or merely into a different kind of busy-ness than we have time for during the week. "The disciples of Christ," he writes, "are asked to avoid any confusion between the celebration of Sunday, which should truly be a way of keeping the Lord's Day holy, and the 'weekend,' understood as a time of simple rest and relaxation." It is this attitude which has, in large part, led to people's widespread distaste for Sundays and the "scaries" they bring along, the anxiety about the coming week which threatens to overwhelm us and reduce us to a "horizon so limited that [we] can no longer see 'the heavens.'"[215]

Fourth, let us put off the hegemony of sports. While Sunday should involve a spirit of play, of fun, all too often we find ourselves

---

[215] Pope John Paul II, *Dies Domini*, no. 4. The concept of "Sunday scaries" was introduced in chapter 1 and is not a term used by the pope.

dedicating the day to sporting events. For many, this looks like rushing out of Mass to make it home in time for whatever more enticing activities await us. For others, especially families with children, it involves rushing from a baseball game to a volleyball game to a recital, with no opportunity for Mass in between. When we make entertainments and contests the focal point of our Sunday, we lose sight of the authentic play to which Christ calls us in the liturgy.

Fifth, let us set aside technology. Our smartphones and laptops threaten always to draw us into menial work. They offer temptations to pornography and masturbation, to frivolous scrolling and frantic shopping, to being everywhere and anywhere but with the Lord and the people He has set before us to love and build up.

While these may seem bold, even unreasonable limitations, they are perhaps quite simple, given the gravity of the mystery and the joy into which the Lord's Day invites us. Leaving off work and chores and setting aside technology may free up a great deal of the time we usually spend on Sunday, and there are a great many activities whereby we can fill the time with more authentic celebration of the Lord.

How to Feast

If we wish to celebrate the Lord's Day well, we should begin to prepare our hearts on Saturday. Saturday evening, rather than a time for parties and entertainments, should be a period of making ready for the Sunday feast. If we use Saturday to complete our work and to prepare our clothes and meals and, most of all, to begin to sow our hearts with the Word, we will find our participation in the liturgy and our enjoyment of the rest of Sunday so much the richer.

Second, we should rise early, like Mary Magdalene and Mary the Mother of God, and go to greet the Lord filled with the joy for which those two holy women could scarcely have hoped on that day beyond the grave. We should attend Mass with clean bodies, neat clothes, and joyful hearts, purified by the sacrament of Confession, eager to hear the Word, hungering and thirsting for the Body of Christ. To this we add that our eucharistic fasts should become again more stringent. Let us greet the Lord empty, if we can, ready to be filled by Him—unless of course our health demands otherwise.

Third, we should eat well, allowing our tables to become joyful extensions of the table of the Lord. We and our children should be nourished bodily with the choicest and most delicious of foods, so that we can rejoice further with God in the goodness of the world and be strengthened to spread that goodness abroad. This demands of us a kind of prodigality, a willingness to be extravagant with our substance in celebration of God's providence.

Fourth, we should perform works of charity. The Lord's Day is a day of freedom, yet many of our brothers and sisters remain cruelly bound by various needs: by hunger and thirst, by poverty and addiction, by cold and heat. St. John Paul II reminds us that "since Apostolic times, the Sunday gathering has in fact been for Christians a moment of fraternal sharing with the very poor."[216] In a stirring passage which can hardly fail to challenge the way many of us spend our Sundays, he goes on:

> From the Sunday Mass there flows a tide of charity destined to spread into the whole life of the faithful, beginning by inspiring the very way in which they live the rest of Sunday. If Sunday is a day of joy, Christians should declare by their actual behaviour that we cannot be happy "on our own."

[216] Ibid., no. 70.

They look around to find people who may need their help. It may be that in their neighbourhood or among those they know there are sick people, elderly people, children or immigrants who precisely on Sundays feel more keenly their isolation, needs and suffering. It is true that commitment to these people cannot be restricted to occasional Sunday gestures. But presuming a wider sense of commitment, why not make the Lord's Day a more intense time of sharing, encouraging all the inventiveness of which Christian charity is capable? Inviting to a meal people who are alone, visiting the sick, providing food for needy families, spending a few hours in voluntary work and acts of solidarity: these would certainly be ways of bringing into people's lives the love of Christ received at the Eucharistic table.[217]

Let us go with Christ on Sundays, then, to heal the sick, feed the hungry, clothe the naked, and give hope to those dwelling on the edge of despair. "God's kingdom is wherever a community is doing justice, where people are reconciled, where people are one in joy," says Ugandan bishop Zac Niringiye.[218] Our Sunday celebration should involve just such justice, such reconciliation, such union in joy.

Fifth, we should enjoy nature. Sunday provides us with an opportunity to rejoice again in the beauty of the natural world and to draw strength from the goodness of God's creation. "As the day on which man is at peace with God, with himself and with others," writes John Paul II, "Sunday becomes a moment when people can

---

[217] Ibid., no. 72.

[218] Quoted in Frank Mulder, "Poor People Don't Need Help," *Plough*, November 14, 2022, https://www.plough.com/en/topics/justice/poor-people-dont-need-help.

look anew upon the wonders of nature, allowing themselves to be caught up in that marvellous and mysterious harmony which, in the words of Saint Ambrose, weds the many elements of the cosmos in 'a bond of communion and peace' by 'an inviolable law of concord and love.' "[219] On Sunday, we learn to look with the eyes of that God who saw that what He had made was good and very good, and we learn to look upon ourselves and our neighbors in this light as well. Such looking shakes off sloth and frees us for the contemplative joy of the one who looks with love on all that is.

Sixth, on the Lord's Day, we should allow our words to be shaped by His Word. It is not enough that we sit in passive inattention as the Word is proclaimed during Mass. Rather, having prepared ourselves beforehand, we should listen with joy to the Word, asking Christ to break it open for us as He did on the road to Emmaus. We should discuss this Word with our families before and after Mass, seeking deeper understanding, seeking to be inflamed for the works of charity. If the Word confuses us, we should seek aid in the commentaries of the saints and in the advice of good priests. When we give ourselves to the Word in this way, we allow our own words to become instruments for building up the Kingdom, and we draw ever nearer the trinitarian heart of all things, where the word of love is breathed among the three holy Persons.

Seventh, we should tithe. Our devotion of time to the Lord should be accompanied with a devotion of our material resources to Him. When we, with Abel the Just and the faithful ones of Israel, give over the first fruits of our labor to God, we create a space of freedom which is part and parcel of true festivity. This kind of extravagance, Josef Pieper argues, creates true freedom because it

[219] Pope John Paul II, *Dies Domini*, no. 67.

proceeds from our own will, a will which turns to the Lord and trusts in Him.[220]

Finally, we should play on the Lord's Day. If there be sports, let them be among families in the backyard or the street, not on the television or in the agitated intensity of the stadium. We should sing and play instruments together. Fathers should wrestle with their little children, and boys and girls should dance to joyful sounds. We should make merry, not because tomorrow we die, but because Christ has died, and tomorrow marks another chance to die with Him and to rise again into that Today that He proclaims in the heavenly liturgy, the day that He has made. Even now, whenever now may be for us, that day is today, the eternal now.

Our age has sought to destroy the Lord's Day. Under the yoke of sloth, we have become sick with ourselves, sick with each other, sick with God. We have given ourselves over to the slavery of the dollar and the slavery of that pharaoh within who seeks to destroy all true worship and to stretch us on the rack of time, ripping us apart between the past and the future so that we can no longer rejoice in the One who is forever present. The Lord's Day teaches us anew to worship, to rejoice, and to be glad. For this is the day that the Lord has made. Let us leave pharaoh behind, go out into the desert, and greet that day with joy.

"Sunday is the proclamation that time, in which he who is the Risen Lord of history makes his home, is not the grave of our illusions but the cradle of an ever new future, an opportunity given to us to turn the fleeting moments of this life into seeds of eternity."[221] By renewing the Lord's Day, by doing so with all

---

[220] Josef Pieper, *Leisure: The Basis of Culture* (1952; repr. San Francisco: Ignatius Press, 2009), 68.

[221] Pope John Paul II, *Dies Domini*, no. 84.

our heart, mind, and soul, we begin to understand the insight of Origen that the perfect Christian "is always in the Lord's Day, and is always celebrating Sunday."[222] We ask the Lord whose day it is to lead us into the light of that celebration, the light of Sinai, the light of Zion, the light of seven days in one, the light of the heavenly Jerusalem where the feast never ends, illuminated by the Lamb who is its lamp.

[222] Ibid., no. 83.

About the Author

Daniel Fitzpatrick lives in New Orleans with his wife and four children. He is the author of the novels *Only the Lover Sings* and *First Make Mad*. His verse translation of the *Divine Comedy*, illustrated by Timothy Schmalz, was published in 2021 in honor of the seven hundredth anniversary of Dante's death.

Daniel is the editor of *Joie de Vivre*, a journal of art, culture, and letters for South Louisiana, and he teaches English at Jesuit High School of New Orleans.

Sophia Institute

Sophia Institute is a nonprofit institution that seeks to nurture the spiritual, moral, and cultural life of souls and to spread the gospel of Christ in conformity with the authentic teachings of the Roman Catholic Church.

Sophia Institute Press fulfills this mission by offering translations, reprints, and new publications that afford readers a rich source of the enduring wisdom of mankind.

Sophia Institute also operates the popular online resource CatholicExchange.com. *Catholic Exchange* provides world news from a Catholic perspective as well as daily devotionals and articles that will help readers to grow in holiness and live a life consistent with the teachings of the Church.

In 2013, Sophia Institute launched Sophia Institute for Teachers to renew and rebuild Catholic culture through service to Catholic education. With the goal of nurturing the spiritual, moral, and cultural life of souls, and an abiding respect for the role and work of teachers, we strive to provide materials and programs that are at once enlightening to the mind and ennobling to the heart; faithful and complete, as well as useful and practical.

Sophia Institute gratefully recognizes the Solidarity Association for preserving and encouraging the growth of our apostolate over the course of many years. Without their generous and timely support, this book would not be in your hands.

www.SophiaInstitute.com
www.CatholicExchange.com
www.SophiaInstituteforTeachers.org

Sophia Institute Press is a registered trademark of Sophia Institute.
Sophia Institute is a tax-exempt institution as defined by the
Internal Revenue Code, Section 501(c)(3). Tax ID 22-2548708.